Scenery

John Hobden

Ian Allan
PUBLISHING

Front cover:
The country railway blended well into its surroundings, and railway activities went on side by side with the rest of everyday life. The M&GN engineers's train heads for Branningham while the harvest is in full swing in the adjoining fields

Previous page:
The Great Western Railway — a part of life at Pendon Parva

Acknowledgements

The late Roye England and Pendon Museum for sowing the seeds of realistic scenery modelling and allowing me to photograph their exhibits.

Fellow scenery creators Gordon and Maggie Gravett, Barry Norman, Allan Downes, Paul Bason and others who have been more than willing to share their techniques with us. We all feed off each other's ideas and improve the breed of scenery modelling.

All those people who have helped in the preparation of this book or who have allowed me to photograph their railways including Don Annison, Bill Davis, Nigel Digby, Conwy Valley Railway Museum, Reg Cooper, Diss M.R.S., Sandy Croall, Malcolm Goodger, Ken de Groome, Peter Kirmond, Barry Norman, Trevor Nunn, Chris Turnbull, Brian Silby, Peter Withers, the various manufacturers who have sent me photos of their products and any others who I may have inadvertently left out.

First published 2010

ISBN 978 0 7110 3510 2

Published by Ian Allan Publishing

an imprint of Ian Allan Publishing Ltd, Hersham, Surrey KT12 4RG.
Printed in England by Ian Allan Printing Ltd, Hersham, Surrey KT12 4RG.

Visit the Ian Allan Publishing website at www.ianallanpublishing.com

Distributed in the United States of America and Canada by BookMasters Distribution Services.

Code 1010/B2

Contents

Introduction

I am not an expert scenery modeller, I am just one of the many who strive for excellence and bow to the work of the masters, several of whose examples appear in these pages.

For me the creation of a model railway entails modelling the whole scene, with the ultimate aim being that the lay person is convinced they are looking at the real thing while the serious enthusiast looks for tell-tale signs that it is a model, such as fishplates in the trackwork and passengers wearing large flat boots. To be convincing, scenery must not be an afterthought. It should be planned as an integral part of the layout and designed to show off the railway models and complement them.

There are sections of this book that are instructional, there are sections that I hope are inspirational, but I hope that the key sections will be those that are challenging and will encourage modellers to find techniques and styles which they are comfortable working with. The techniques described can be used by anyone, though they will be familiar to many experienced modellers who may find more of interest in the philosophy of scenic modelling.

It was my first visit to Pendon Museum as a teenager that got me started on scenery modelling, first in 4mm scale with London & South Western Railway scenes (*Railway Modeller*, September 1979) and later in 7mm scale with the Midland & Great Northern Joint Railway, near where I live. Though most of the photographs are of models in these scales, the techniques transfer to any scale.

As you create a fully scenic model railway even fictitious places take on a life of their own, and you find yourself almost living in the landscape! Making the landscape will take you to places noone has ever seen before and can be a most rewarding experience.

I have learnt so much more about scenery modelling as a result of analysing the work of others during the course of writing, that I now want to re-work most of my own railway which has already taken 30 years to create!

John Hobden, Downham Market, Norfolk, 2010

Norfolk cottages at West Runton. In the 1930s the nurse would visit by bicycle.

building. My friend and I had cycled 50 miles to find we were the only visitors and were honoured to be given the full works by Roye England, the founder of the Museum. Pendon Museum also houses one of the early 4mm:ft scale scenic layouts, The 'Madder Valley Railway', created by John Ahern. While nothing like as detailed as the main Pendon exhibits, it shows attention to detail and a consistency of standards and colour.

Most model railways are built to showcase the railway element and include only sufficient landscape to set the scene, period and atmosphere.

Many model railways, especially in the larger scales, have precious little room for large scale scenery once track has been laid and therefore rely on a number of design tricks to give the illusion that there is much more of the non railway world in the model than there really is. Flat backgrounds and low relief buildings help to add more of the world beyond the railway without eating up precious baseboard space.

It is not necessary to include the whole height of a feature where its size can be conveyed by pruning out less essential parts or simply by shrinking a little. Allan

In hilly areas the railway has to thread its way through, taking the easiest route. No 66525 with its train of hopper wagons is dwarfed by the hills as it crosses Dent Head Viaduct on the Settle and Carlisle line on 9 September 2009.

The low relief buildings used here on the Diss MRS layout 'Billington' say 'This is in a town', yet cost only inches of baseboard space. The buildings are all commercial offerings yet they are consistent and well blended together.

Downes, whose writing has appeared many times in the *Railway Modeller* and *Model Rail* over the years, manages to create elaborate models of grand historical buildings which announce their importance in the scene without taking it over.

Very few stations are modelled exactly to scale as they would simply not fit in the available space and so they are compressed horizontally into a smaller space by shortening sidings and gaps between features. Some vertical compression is also possible and can be applied to hills and to trees.

It is well worth trying out ideas by sketching the relationships between various features of your proposed scenes and then making a rough mock-up to test the ideas. Big hills can be simulated by blankets draped over chairs and buildings can be simulated by cardboard boxes. It is possible to create mock-up buildings in paper or card quite quickly and this is the method used by Nigel Digby to gain an impression of how a scene will look. At this stage ask what the scene will look like from different angles. Only when you are happy with this can you go on to plan in detail.

Styles of scenery

It might be argued that there are 'schools' of scenery creators in the same way as there are genres in music and art.

Some of the most effective railways are created in the form of a closed diorama. In this style the railway has a frame which acts as a focus for the picture inside, rather like the proscenium arch of a traditional theatre. In the theatre the house lights are dimmed and the stage lights bright. This cannot be achieved in an exhibition setting so many modellers create a dark surround to the model and provide its own lighting system which is brighter than the hall lights. The late Jack Nelson was a master of this style of scenery and fortunately several of his dioramas can be viewed at the Conwy Railway Museum at Betws-y-Coed in North Wales. Jack did not have the benefit of many of the materials we now use but still managed to create masterpieces using artistic techniques. Jack's scenes were not operating railways and indeed some could not have been, featuring track which became narrower gauge as it went away from the observer.

At home we have more opportunity to control the lighting and so we can direct light towards the model and use dark curtains to mask the area below the baseboard. My own curtains are made of black ground cover fabric from the local garden centre.

Another popular device which works well on urban railways is to frame the scene using a tall building such as a warehouse or factory. This also does away

Opposite top left: The late Jack Nelson used perspective in ways which are not usually available to normal modellers. In this scene the carriage is built in perspective and the rails narrow as they go away from the observer. But this scene is extremely evocative of the LNWR which was Jack's love. These dioramas were first featured in the Railway Modeller magazine in the 1960s and were due to be revisited by the same magazine during 2010.

Above right: 'Zweiburg', in Z gauge by Brian Silby. This very effective diorama style layout uses some perspective but is fully operable. The viewer's attention is concentrated on the scene by the black surround.

Centre right: In this scene the vehicles on the nearer viaduct are built in perspective at about 10mm:ft scale while the rear viaduct is a standard 4mm:ft scale line. Where a viewing window such as the viaduct is provided there is no reason why a normal model should not employ these techniques.

Right: 'Crumley & Little Wickhill' (Hull MRS) takes the diorama idea even further by almost immersing the viewer in the scene, in this case a valley between two hills.

with the need for background scenery. Part of the art form seems to lie in the creation of factory names which are a play on words, such as 'Curlup & Dye, Hair Care Products'. Some railways are constructed to showcase particular operations on the railway such as a locomotive shed or shunting yard. Very effective and lively scenes have been created with a factory or quarry as their *raison d'être*.

In the smaller scales there have been several layouts set in hilly country which feature very large hills and at exhibitions the operators can just be seen peering over the hills. The Manchester Model Railway Society layout 'Chee Tor' was one of the early examples in 2mm:ft scale and really gave the impression of the Peak District landscape it was meant to traverse. A very unusual hybrid between the diorama and the hilly layout has been created by members of Hull Model Railway Society. This is 'Crumley & Little Wickhill', where viewers look through the valley between the hills to see the railway.

Quayside scenes have always been popular as they give the opportunity to incorporate another dimension through the inclusion of another transport system. Tramways give a similar effect, and can be operated by giving the current supply through the rails. Moving cars have been incorporated into railway layouts and work well when driven by magnetic means that do not intrude into the scene, unlike a few in the 1960s where the Scalextric or Minic Motorway-type tracks were embedded in the road! More recently the Faller road system uses self-propelled vehicles following a wire embedded in the road.

'Elmwell Village' depot shows its winter 1950s face, near to the time of the line's closure. For this rotating layout, Brian Jenkins had to build the shop four times in its different guises! Photo by Tony Wright, courtesy British Railway Modelling

Your choice of scenery style and your prototype will probably be guided more by considerations of the space available, whether you want to move the layout to exhibit it and your personal skill levels (unless you have friends or a club to call on). If your layout is intended for exhibition you may want to consider a layout with an unusual theme such as the seasonal variation seen on 'Elmwell Village Depot'. This railway, which is now on permanent exhibition at the Historical Model Railway Society centre at Butterley is constructed to rotate so that four separate sections depict a variation in the seasons and in the period modelled, varying between spring in the 1900s to winter in the 1950s. An exhibit such as this will keep viewers interested for longer as there is the anticipation of changes of scene as well as interest in the different items of locomotives and rolling stock which pass along the line.

Making scenery believable

In the heyday of the railways travel was more leisurely and the style of decoration was elaborate. Cromer Beach in 1920 still has all its Edwardian features.

In the theatre the scenery department uses very simple means to create the illusion of a sense of place which transports the audience far from Leicester Square, Newcastle or Broadway. Artists use perspective, fading colours and foils to lead the eye to the foreground while creating the background in a way that stops us focusing on it. A very small number of modellers are also able to do this with a few flicks of a paintbrush. I am not one of them and this book is for the majority who need to follow a formula to create something believable.

There is an expression 'suspension of disbelief' which sums up the authentic railway modeller's craft. I assert that all our modelling efforts are steeped in nostalgia, whether for an age gone by or for a believable re-creation of the modern scene. My friend Chris Turnbull has a model of the same station as I do. The main difference is that his model is set in the present or very recent past. He has a supermarket where I have a goods yard and no sooner has a new operating company been awarded a franchise then he is on the phone or writing letters to get details of their exact livery and drawings of their rolling stock. To me that is as much historical modelling as my research into the early 20th century. I enjoy watching and operating his railway as it transports me to a different place and time just as a television drama takes us all out of our familiar circumstances and into a world of make-believe. The 'victims' who come to operate my railway are subjected to reading Special Notices in the language of the 1920s and '30s while the atmosphere of 2009 is re-created on a modern image line by 'The delayed 13.30 First Capital Connect service to Brighton will depart from platform one...' and by figures on the lineside in Hi-Vis jackets tending to broken overhead lines.

The key to being able to suspend disbelief lies in ensuring that everything in the scene could have been there at the same time and that no component of the scene clashes with another. This means avoiding sudden changes in texture or colour and ensuring consistency throughout. John Ahern's 'Madder Valley Railway' exhibited at Pendon Museum is nowhere near as detailed as the main Pendon exhibits and lacks the range of textures available to modern modellers but its consistency makes the scene so very believable. The modern preservation movement has distorted the bounds of authenticity somewhat but generally a Ford

By 2005 everything in the scene has been modernised. Though the 'Arts and Crafts'-style station building is still in existence it is now a restaurant and the trains drop their passengers at a minimal platform with the new supermarket as a backdrop. This scene, created by Chris Turnbull, is every bit as evocative of its age as the earlier one on the author's railway.

Cortina car will look out of place in a railway goods yard alongside horse-drawn carts and private owner wagons. Television producers spend a lot of time researching such things and their work provides a useful short cut and some inspiration for our efforts. Enthusiasts scour programmes for 'slip-ups'. The classic example comes from the television series 'Flambards' from the 1980s which featured actors supposedly from the 19th century riding through stubble fields which clearly showed evidence of harvesting by combine harvester followed by burning of the rows of straw. The Victorians never burnt straw as it was too valuable a commodity to be wasted. But yet, we forgive those film makers who do the best they can with the resources available and who try to re-create the main line to Exeter by filming on the Severn Valley Railway!

There are many useful books on earlier ways of life which provide rich sources of material on which we can base our scenery. The 19th century is particularly well covered, while the 1930s is sparse. Guide books from the 1950s and '60s are available and local studies libraries and their librarians can be a rich resource.

There is an odd anomaly in the world of railway modelling, or perhaps more correctly in the world of collectables, and that is in the creation of authentic historical scenes, not of real railways but of toy trains from days gone by. Collectors of Hornby O gauge clockwork, Basset Lowke and Hornby Dublo three-rail strive to re-create not an accurate prototypical scene but one of the living rooms or sheds of the 1930s, '50s or '60s. For these collectors the scene is not complete without an authentic Hornby tunnel, platform and station building. A Hornby tunnel was little more than a mottled green papier mâché semi-circle to place over a short section of track but to a nine year old in the 1950s it was Primrose Hill, Box or Woodhead. Accurate representations of a particular prototype would be out of place here but stylised scenes in keeping with the style of the commercial offerings of the time can create a very effective background to what was in essence an artist's impression of reality.

Capturing the essence of the period

The immaculate Midland Johnson Single of 1899 was an elegant masterpiece in a world where labour was cheap and the streets and

countryside were kept in a similar style by armies of labourers. Apart from the wildest countryside in the remote hills the whole landscape was tended and neat. Even in the 1950s the vegetation of the roadside verges and railway cuttings was cut regularly by hand by labourers using a sickle or grasshook. The scythe used to cut corn or hay was too big for this job. It was this process which kept the banks neat. In the 1960s the absence of this regular cutting allowed brambles to grow and by the 1970s small trees abounded. By the 1980s railway cuttings were copses and at the end of the 20th century leaves on the line were so common as to spawn jokes when announcements about delayed trains referred to them.

In earlier periods many more people could be seen walking in the vicinity of the railway line. In the week these were workers but at weekends ordinary people would be out looking at the trains as they passed.

A few railway modellers set their period at an exact date; for example Pendon Museum sets itself at August 1912. Many others like to set a wider period, say from 1920 to 1939, in order to be able to run a wider variety of stock. In constructing scenery it is useful to be able to set a scene in which nothing is out of place. Many aspects of British and European scenery are almost timeless. Fields, hedgerows and older buildings change little over centuries, but introduce something completely out of period and the illusion can be destroyed.

Platform edges were hand painted with whitewash until the 1960s, another job for porter Peggy Pooley c1945. M&GN Circle MGN-PWS-0354

This scene, typical of the Victorian and Edwardian railway scene, shows a well-maintained, graceful locomotive, moving through carefully tended surroundings. An army of labourers was required to maintain this standard. Jack Braithwaite collection

Detail from a typical Ordnance Survey 25in to the mile plan. For most purposes the features shown on these plans will be adequate.

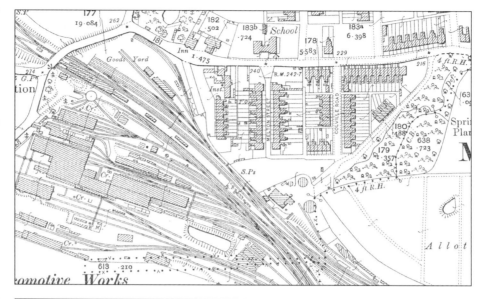

If available an official 1:500 survey may give additional details such as switch and crossing layout.

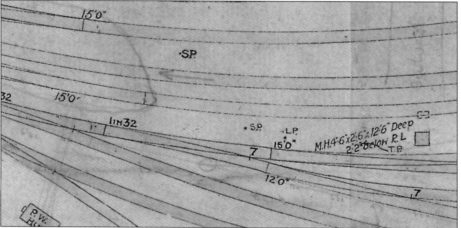

It is natural to want to run locomotives and stock from different periods and so it is wise to consider which aspects of scenery have not changed and even to consider changing certain items when running earlier or later stock. Vehicles are easy to change, station buildings change little but the dress of passengers can be remarkably different over the years. I have always glued my poor subjects to the platform but in writing this book I have had cause to reconsider — perhaps I should drill up their legs and insert wires so I can plant them on the platform without gluing them down.

I personally find it most useful to become immersed in the period and district that I am modelling. Visits to your chosen area are useful even if you are modelling a freelance scene but for those who cannot visit then there are many excellent albums of historical photographs, not only depicting railways but also the everyday life of the people who created the man-made landscape of the times. In these days of the 'information superhighway' much of this research may be carried out by reference to websites run by local communities.

When planning a railway based on a specific location a most useful document to obtain is a large scale Ordnance Survey plan. These are available from www.old-maps.co.uk for various dates and show track plans as at the date of survey and every fence, hedge, signal post and building. Even better, if you can get one, is the railway company's own survey, usually at a scale of 1:500 and showing every detail of the railway's equipment. Many line societies have these available, either singly or as bound booklets.

Being consistent

Nothing will destroy any illusions we try to create more than an obvious change of style, texture or level of detail. One of the great strengths of John Ahern's 'Madder Valley Railway', on display at Pendon Museum, is that similar, subtle colours are used throughout. Its level of detail is less than we would expect these days but it still manages to transport viewers back to an earlier age and to a leisurely, rural way of life.

Using all the techniques available to 21st century modellers we need to ensure that materials used, for example to create grassy meadows, are compatible with those used to create parklands unless a stark change is needed to emphasise a change in the landscape itself. If carpet underlay is used for rough grass on a hillside then it should also be used for rough grass in the nearby town. The contrast needed to show neatly tended lawns or even well-grazed sheep paths can be created using finer flock powders but with a transition if appropriate.

When creating buildings materials and techniques should be chosen with consistency in mind. Only when it is necessary to draw viewers' attention to the contrast between, say, an ancient building and a brash new station should changes in materials and finishes be considered.

'East Lynn', beautifully crafted by Trevor Nunn, is not just a model railway. It is a re-creation of the whole commercial economy of the 19th century. At exhibitions this style of layout attracts interest from whole families, especially when exhibited in the area from which the real buildings were drawn — King's Lynn, Norfolk.

Returning to the work of Jack Nelson, this scene shows the consistency referred to above and confirms how Jack had immersed himself in the culture of the heyday of the LNWR.

Hills, dales, slopes and cliffs

Ribblehead viaduct is huge if you are standing beneath it but this shot shows LMS No 5690 Leander dwarfed by the hills as it crosses the viaduct on the Settle and Carlisle line on 9 September 2009.

Acompanion volume in the 'Aspects of Modelling' series covers baseboard construction in detail and so we will be concerned here only with the design of the shape of the baseboards to accommodate the landscape. The decision on baseboard type will be greatly influenced by any needs for deep valleys with viaducts or bridges. For portable and exhibition lines we must decide whether any scenery needs to be removed for transport and incorporate fixing methods into the design. Do we need to be able to lean on scenery to carry out maintenance?

The shape of the land in relation to our railways

Railways in hilly locations need rather more space to be convincing. Some N gauge railways are able to take large tracts of baseboard to create the hills that the line runs through, but even these cannot match the sheer size of real hills. Even the rolling hills of the South Downs, where the Brighton line tunnels through tower some 400ft (122m) above the railway. For 2mm:ft scale that's 800mm. Parts of the Settle and Carlisle line lie 1,000ft (305m) below the surrounding hills; that's a massive 6ft 6in (2m) above the rails in 2mm scale. But in actual fact we do not need such huge hills to create the impression of high ground. We will believe they are higher than their scale height if they have all the other characteristics of hilly country and we can even use perspective by making features such as trees smaller in the background to enhance the impression of distance.

The late Jack Nelson (*Railway Modeller* 1965) created scenes in this way as seen in Chapter 1. With really big scenes it may be worth trying to fade the colour of the landscape to a more grey/blue shade. I have not seen this in practice but it could work.

The number one rule in creating the ground that our railways run through is to consider what was there before the railway. Land is solid and its shape is decided by its geology. This same geology often determines the economy of an area and is sometimes responsible for the coming of the railway in the first place. Coalfields and ironstone quarries were opened up by railways and the industrial and transport infrastructure were inextricably linked to give these areas their character. Where the economic need was great the railways found ways to get to otherwise inaccessible places. Devices such as rope-worked inclines (Cromford & High Peak) and narrow gauge lines where sharp curves could hug mountainsides brought out the fruits of the mines and quarries.

Hard rocks tend to produce steeper slopes than soft ones, though this is not universal. In the southeast of England the landscape consists generally of rolling hills but where there were no convenient gaps such as river valleys the railways cut deep cuttings and tunnels through them, not to give the navvies practice in the use of the tunnelling shield but to get the most efficient line between stations. Valleys were followed where possible, but cutting through chalk or clay was relatively cheap when labour was freely available. In the southwest of England, the Pennines, Wales, Scotland, the Alps and other mountainous areas of the world the cost of digging or blasting away huge quantities of rock meant selection of routes which followed valleys or other gentle routes. Narrow gauge railways could use sharper curves, making it easier to follow the sides of valleys and so they were favoured in Wales, where slates were transported by rail to the ports, and in the Rockies where minerals were moved by railroads such as the Durango & Silverton and the Georgetown Loop.

It made sense to use the spoil from cuttings to make embankments and only to construct tunnels and viaducts where it was essential. On our models we may use either to help create our illusion but if we do we must make their use believable and necessary. A tunnel can be a very useful scenic break but if we use it as such we need to make it look as if there was a real reason for digging through the hill rather than skirting round it. There were a few places where tunnels were constructed when they were not necessary, usually when a landowner wanted the railway through his land to be concealed. This even happens today, as when the M25 motorway round London was constructed and a tunnel was built to avoid disturbing a cricket pitch in Essex.

Many model railways are built with a flat base, broken only by water features. These usually need higher areas for hills etc and these can either be built from solid material such as insulation foam or a series of card or ply profiles covered in cloth (or grass matt), card or Mod Roc (plaster-impregnated cloth which sets solid when wetted). This can even be supported on lumps of screwed-up newspaper but the result will not bear much weight and is difficult to control the shape of. An ingenious system of creating support for hills is based on the use of empty plastic

Blea Moor, built by Peter Kirmond, illustrates how the model landscape can be created to show the railway cutting through it. The rough grass, typical of the Pennine moorland, is created from lint on very light formers and forms a steep backdrop to the railway, so that only a light blue sky curtain is needed to complete the scene.

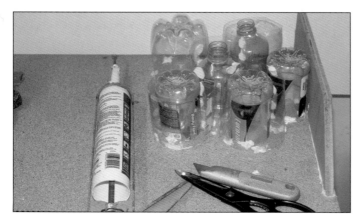

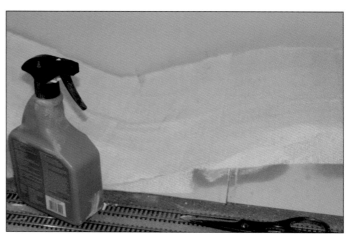

Top left: A cheap yet remarkably strong foundation to your hill scene can be achieved with plastic drinks bottles, a pair of scissors and a hot glue gun or 'hard as nails'.

Top right: The conventional approach to hill construction uses parallel formers cut from ply.

Centre left: Strips of card across the top of ply formers or drinks bottles form the base for the soil or foliage layer.

Centre right: Mod Roc sheets are draped over the card strips and may be wetted in a bowl of water or my preference is to spray them with water then smooth them over with fingers. Warning: It gets messy from here on so either work in a shed or cover everything that you don't want to become coated in plaster dust and spillages!

Bottom left: Small amounts of finishing plaster or Artex can be mixed in any bowl with a little PVA added along with brown poster or powder paint. This can be bought in bulk from educational suppliers.

Bottom right: Spoon it on and smooth out with a brush or card scraper.

drinks bottles. Rings are cut from the bottles and stuck to the baseboard close together using a hot glue gun. The tops are coated with PVA and Mod Roc or grass mats are laid over them. More strength can be added by using additional layers of Mod Roc or any material coated in plaster or Artex. Add some dark coloured powder or poster paint to this mix so that if the ground is chipped later it appears as soil and not as white plaster. An advantage to thicker scenery created like this is that it is easier to drill through to give a good foundation to fences and trees. (Try sticking fence posts upright into a single layer of grass mat!)

An even easier way to create hills and dales is to use foam insulation boards as used in the building industry. The PIR foam type are the best, being quite dense enough to bear your weight as you lean over to attend to something on the far side of the baseboard, yet fairly easy to shape using simple tools such as the kitchen bread knife. Some modellers have used expanded polystyrene boards and moulded them using a spade bit on a soldering iron. This is effective but generates toxic fumes. Also, polystyrene is a little soft for leaning on. The disadvantage to using these boards is that they come in set thicknesses and it is difficult to get smoothly curving slopes typical of hillsides. It may be tempting to cut them with a saw but only do this if you enjoy hoovering up minute pieces of polystyrene that will find their way into everything for weeks!

Foam board needs careful trimming and you will need a long blade for smooth cuts. It may look like the family bread knife, but please don't tell.

Geology is mentioned above and it is well worth studying the landforms of the area you wish to portray before deciding on a system for creating them. Where the land is made of hard rocks such as sandstone, granite and limestone there may be very steep slopes with rocky outcrops but where it is of clay or chalk the outlines are smooth where the rocks have been worn away over many thousands of years. In clay lands every valley will have a stream through the bottom but in chalk and limestone country many valleys are dry.

As we choose the most appropriate system for creating the surface of the earth through which our railways run the underlying rock will probably be the main determinant in this. For gently undulating scenery in clay or loose sand a baseboard which has a flat surface will probably be most appropriate. For harder rocks such as chalk, sandstone or granite a system based on layers of expanded or extruded foam will probably be more suitable.

We want our scenery to make the point about it being a hilly, mountainous or flat location and, surprisingly, if we follow the exact contours and heights of our chosen prototype location we do not get an effect which matches the impression we get when actually walking around the site. We need to use a device used by the British Geological Survey when preparing their maps. This is known as 'vertical exaggeration' and is a process by which the highs and lows are exaggerated to match our visual perception of the same scene. I suppose the same effect is achieved by using horizontal compression so it is probably best to use trial and error with mock-up scenery until we are happy with the general effect.

Ken de Groome's 'Rickmansworth' railway bursts out of its shed at this point and the bridge provides the scenic break.

Another key element in the design of baseboard and choice of system is the way you wish to portray your railway. You may want to have a junction station with one branch disappearing behind the scenes while another continues in front, each going to its own fiddle yard or to the same one, or perhaps a continuous run. This may entail splitting the backscene to allow the branch to exit the visible part of the railway.

There are many devices, tricks and illusions that can be used to allow a part of the railway to exit discretely. Some classics include an overbridge, usually with a feature to draw the eye away from the fact that there is a flat backscene on one side of the bridge. A rival company's line with a signal or a locomotive is perhaps the best but a bridge with a street lamp or bus can be equally effective.

Simply splitting the backscene can be effective, but again needs some interest to draw the eye.

When creating the earthworks through which and on which our railway runs there are some basic guidelines to follow. As the navvies removed earth and rock from cuttings and tunnels it was carted away to fill the hollows and simply tipped out of carts until it achieved the correct height for the formation. Materials tipped

The bridge need not be too grand as this example shows. Lord Rothermere's footbridge near Holt in Norfolk is surrounded by trees. The model is on the author's 'Norfolk Joint Railway' and arrests the viewer's eye as the main line heads for the fiddle yard. The timbers are crossing timbers from an American model railroad supplier.

Cork bark makes very effective weathered limestone and soft sandstone.

Woodland Scenics rock mould is designed for use with plaster compounds. Mixing in an amount of water-based or powder paint makes it self colouring.

Attacking the foam building board with a wire brush was just an experiment which was nearly abandoned at this stage.

like this never make a slope with greater than a 45 degree angle and most slopes made like this are about 40 degrees. Cuttings, on the other hand, can be much steeper and almost vertical in the case of solid rock but much less in unstable clay. In clay, sand and sometimes chalk the sides of cuttings are smooth and for that reason I prefer to construct them in thick card (the sort that is found on the back of sketch books seems ideal and can be cut with a Stanley knife).

Rocks are difficult to make convincingly. For many years the standard method was to use cork bark and this gives a fair impression of a nondescript general kind of rock. Layers of insulation foam board make a fair impression of sedimentary rocks such as sandstone, limestone and chalk. Study photographs of the real thing as usual and vary the thickness of the layers. Chalk is composed of thinner layers than most rocks but this varies throughout the area where chalk may be found from the Yorkshire Wolds, through Hertfordshire, Kent and into Dorset. In some locations the layers of rocks are nowhere near horizontal so if your chosen location needs this effect it is probably best to build the layers horizontally and glue them to the sides of the cutting at the required angle, trimming off at top and bottom. Harder rocks are more angular and are best made using a soft plastic mould such as those sold by Woodland Scenics. These use a plaster-based compound for the rocks and again the tip is to incorporate some water-based colour (acrylic is OK) so that any chips do not stand out. When the rock is set it is removed from the mould and painted a base colour appropriate to the type of rock. Next apply lighter and darker shades in a mottled pattern or in lines to simulate bedding. There is almost always vegetation growing in cracks in rocks and sometimes quite large trees jut out from the surface.

Some modellers have managed to create rather realistic rocks using the insulation boards mentioned above. This involves carving rock shapes and can be quite effective. I couldn't get on with this method but I did try making rocks by distressing the insulation boards. I used a sharp knife to make cuts parallel to the ground at irregular intervals to represent the bedding of the rocks. The same knife was jabbed into the beds of rock, again at irregular intervals. I then scoured the whole lot with a wire brush quite vigorously. Same warning here about the tiny bits of dust that were produced — do it outdoors and let the wind blow it onto your neighbours' washing! At this stage I was not convinced but I persevered and gave it a wash with dilute PVA to seal the open pores in the material. I gave it a quick blow over with the airbrush while I was spraying the ballast with track colour and suddenly it looked okay. A couple of lines of small stones gathered from a Welsh roadside pressed into the rock to simulate a bed of harder rock and I was convinced. I think it might even make effective chalk if sprayed white then washed with dark grey to emphasise the joints in the rock. Most rock faces, as mentioned above, have plants growing on them so a few strands of foliage net finished off the scene.

Real sandstone rocks beside the railway line at Trehafod, Gwent. These hard rocks need the Woodland Scenics mould treatment.

Buildings

This Midland Railway station building at Wellingborough is in red brick with yellow and blue brick detail, typical of the district.

Buildings deserve a book to themselves and several have been written. This is where precision really does meet artistry. There are a few true artists who can model buildings freehand and who can incorporate exaggerations and caricatures into them. Most of us need some form of guidance such as a kit if one is available or a drawing or measurements. Whatever system you choose it is important to go for consistency and try to avoid anything which is out of place such as a brightly coloured roof on an otherwise dull coloured building. Hours spent studying real buildings and photographs will be repaid in the quality of your models.

You may think that if you model a prototype location you can just make models of all the buildings, put them in the right places and you have an authentic model. Authentic, yes, but effective in transporting the viewer to that place and time? How much of the scene do we need to actually create to achieve our purpose? Could we create low- or half-relief buildings as a backdrop against the backscene or even use photographs of the real thing as our background? But more of that later.

If we are creating a fictitious scene then we need to study typical examples and ask what kinds of buildings we will need to complete the scene. A station building is usually expected unless our scene is a locomotive shed or yard scene. Most companies had their own typical styles built in certain years and often adapted them to suit local building materials and styles.

The main station building was frequently located nearest to the settlement it was meant to serve and a lesser platform shelter was often found on the opposite platform of a two- or three-platform station.

A goods shed was a feature of most country stations and some had separate lamp rooms, weighbridge huts, granaries or fish stores.

Some original stations have been demolished to make way for bland but functional structures which serve today's needs more efficiently but here at Wellingborough the ancient canopy still performs its original function. The cast iron columns and ornamental spandrels will still be there long after the HST has been recycled.

Bottom left: Downham Market station in Norfolk uses the local 'carrstone', an iron-rich sandstone.

Below: Wansford station on the Nene Valley Railway was built by the London & Birmingham Railway (later London & North Western Railway) but in similar style to prominent local buildings. The same is true of Stamford East, a few miles away but built by the Great Northern Railway. Any shelter for passengers has been removed.

Dent Station, further up the Midland Railway, uses local millstone grit as its building material.

Other buildings adjacent to the station can create an impression of the kind of settlement the station served. Factory buildings will say one thing about your railway while thatched cottages will say another. It was very common for the land between the town and the railway to be filled with terraced houses (see below) but the side presented to the travelling public was usually the rear of the houses.

At an early stage in the design of your railway you will need to decide how you want viewers to see the railway in context. Presenting the station with goods yard in front, then station and town behind is probably the most common but can be difficult for operating manual couplings at an exhibition. For a railway at home, especially one in a loft, you can surround yourself and have one scene on one side and another opposite.

Left: Stamford East in 7mm scale by Tony Sparks, built in ply and card over 30 years ago.

Below left: Do all early railway stations have these ornate gables? Stone, Staffs.

Below right: Station architecture followed patterns, often with the same design being constructed in different materials. This Great Western Railway stone station building is at Aynho, between Oxford and Banbury.

Left: Lesser stations had less imposing buildings as here at West Runton in Norfolk. A ticket office and a waiting room were the only essential requirements. This structure is in card with plastic facing and aluminium representation of corrugated iron roof.

The platform shelter built by the Great Western Railway at King's Sutton near Banbury is typical of many. Network Rail have chosen blue instead of the original cream for the valence but otherwise it is as built.

Cromer Beach goods yard also boasted a granary building, constructed in timber and sharing a road with the brick-built goods shed. The slate roofing is described later in this chapter. This scene also illustrates a minimal backscene.

Below left: If your railway is set in the days before the tumble dryer then you could set the day of the week by stringing lines of washing from the backs of these terraced houses (from Northampton) to represent Monday (did they get covered in smuts?). Some of the windows here are still set back into the brickwork while modern replacements are almost flush.

Creating regional styles and period housing to suit your railway

Most modellers start with a pretty good idea of the district they want their model to be set in and some areas can be re-created with very simple but typical examples of the local vernacular. Terraced houses can be found all over the UK but, although they were mainly built during the latter half of the 19th century to similar designs, regional variations give them distinct characters. Terraces on different sides of the Pennines might be built of the same millstone grit under slate roofs but those in Accrington differ markedly from those in Huddersfield.

Colour and texture are very important in giving buildings their character. Most building materials take their colour from the natural materials they are made from and so the colours of burnt clay and natural stone or slate predominate. Experiment with a range of colours and compare with photographs until you get the effect you want. Also enlist others to give a second opinion. Remember there is a wide variety in the colours of even a factory mass-produced brick so don't expect a sheet of plastic bricks painted all the same colour to look realistic. You may get away with painting all the same base colour to start with but expect to

paint a large number individually or in groups with other shades. Colours which look intense in full size can appear overpowering if you paint your model in the exact same shade. For example, I find that the best colour to use as a base for light red bricks is actually a salmon colour (I use London & South Western Railway coach salmon). Test pieces can help to a certain degree.

Also consider the effects of different kinds of lighting — fluorescent tubes can give a sickly greenish hue to buildings and this effect can only partially be offset by using daylight types.

Sloping roofed terrace in Colne, Lancs, compared with stepped homes in West Yorkshire only 20 miles away.

A typical pair of Victorian semis in southeast England. Terraces are smaller but are similar in looks.

Street elevation

Rear elevation

Victorian terraced houses

Side elevation

Side Elevation   Front Elevation

1950s Semi-detached Bungalows

Semi detached 'local authority' houses

Above left: These terraced houses are easy to build from kits or scratchbuild. They can also be useful as background scenes for which we shall return to them later.

Above centre: Models set in more recent times will feature buildings of the period. This style of building was popular in the 1950s.

Above: Many local authority houses were built in small estates from the 1930s to 1970s. There is a similarity of style shared by many of them.

Left: In country areas houses were often built singly and the gaps filled later when land became short. Note the large stone lintels on these examples from Alston in Cumbria.

Kits or scratchbuilt? ..... or commission an expert?

It is possible to put together a convincing model railway using the range of building kits available and if your line does not follow a particular prototype this is a quick way forward. Card kits such as Superquick and Bilteezi can be made to produce convincing buildings if constructed with care. Small details such as chimneys are best added from solid tubes etc rather than try to make the rolled card as supplied in the kits.

Most of the card building kits were designed in the 1950s and '60s, are perfect for railways set in that era, and rather nostalgic for the author whose early railways relied heavily on these offerings — two shillings (10p) each or one week's pocket money. Alphagraphix joined the established ranges in the 1980s with several generic building types. All card kits need to be braced or stuck onto stiffer card backing to prevent the walls and roof bowing. Plastic and resin buildings are more substantial but need to be carefully painted in matt colours and weathered to look convincing. Townstreet resin cast buildings bring relief into play and can be very convincing if well painted.

American outline modellers have some exquisite building kits available, including the Ragg's to Riches range available from NGTrains in York.

Hornby's Skaledale range can be made to look realistic if carefully placed in a scene and they offer a wide range of generic buildings which could very quickly create a suitable background for the railway. There are possibilities for customising by cutting, joining and combining various parts.

These commercial offerings are fine for a freelance layout or if you find they fit, or can be customised to fit, a real location you want to model. But if you decide to build a particular prototype then you have little alternative but to scratchbuild. Don't panic, it's not that difficult and your most important tool is your eyes.

Where shall we start? Well, let's choose our subject and see how big it is and how we might construct it.

Left: A generic locomotive shed built from a Superquick kit by Charlie Warren.

Below: These buildings were constructed using two Bilteezi kits. A great variety of individual buildings can be created by adapting the various parts. Care has been taken to touch in any exposed card at the folds. Jerry Freestone (Freestone Model Accessories)

*Below: Hornby
Skaledale East station
building has a flavour o
the Settle and Carlisle
to it as do all of this
range.* **Manufacturer's
photo**

Sources of measurements and drawings

For railway buildings the easiest source of information is the relevant line society. Most have drawings of the buildings on their lines and are willing to sell copies. These will generally be at scales which do not suit our models and so we will need to re-scale them. A good photocopier will do this, in sections if necessary. There may be occasions when it is useful to make the model at a slightly smaller scale than our railway, for example if the building is in the background or, as in my case, when I did not physically have the space to fit in the full size station building at Cromer. Railway company drawings are often at a scale of ¼in to the foot or 1:48, not too far out for O gauge at 7mm:ft or 1:43. Another dodge for making a building smaller is to leave out a bay or room to shorten it. Beware of making it narrower without lowering the height as that could make it look out of proportion.

If you do not have access to a drawing and the building is still in existence you can measure it yourself. Do ask permission from the owners first! This measuring activity can be useful in more ways than one. You will attract attention to yourself and there may be interested onlookers who could come and share their memories of the old railway. All that you need for measuring is a long tape (30m) from B&Q etc and a supply of post-it notes to write the measurements on. You can stick the post-it to the tape to save carrying a clipboard. Take lots of photos as well as you are bound to forget to measure something and you can estimate distances by counting bricks. Most railway buildings used four brick courses to 1ft (305mm) and bricks were 4in (101mm) wide by 8½in (216mm) long. Many windows were standard sizes such as 3ft (915mm) or 4ft (1.225m) wide by 3ft 6in (1.05m) up to 5ft (1.5m) deep.

Having got your shorthand measurements, sketches and photos back at base the next job is to transfer them to paper (or computer if you have suitable CAD software). I use CAD nowadays (download free software from http://www.cadstd.com/lite.html) but for many years I used an A3 drawing board as illustrated.

First draw a base line and mark all the horizontal measurements along it. Using the set square, extend these upwards as parallel lines then mark the horizontal lines which form the tops and bottoms of the windows and doors. Go over in ink with a fine-pointed pen to firm up the window openings etc. If you have gables and chimneys, draw them in using the brick-counting method to get the height and width. Do this for each elevation (side view). You may wish to draw a plan view too. You now have a basic working drawing. You can transfer this to your chosen wall-making material by hand or using the parallel motion on the drawing board or even cheat by photocopying and sticking down onto your wall board.

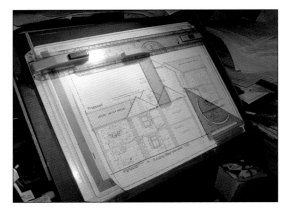

At this stage you could photocopy your building drawing onto thin card to make a mock-up to see how it fits into the scene. Nigel Digby hand tints his very effectively which quickly adds more realism and gives almost the effect of a Superquick or Bilteezi kit. If working on a computer you could enhance this effect by pasting in images from real photographs of brick or stonework, possibly even windows. If you do this try to get your photos from as far away as possible and zoom in with the camera to reduce the distortion which inevitably comes with using a wide angle lens.

A typical student's A3 drawing board with parallel rule and set square. I made the angled stand from MDF, it makes using the board so much more comfortable.

Constructing Model Buildings: Brick walls

Brickwork is an advanced craft with its own terminology which is worthy of study. Brick walls are built in such a way that they remain stable and do not collapse in extreme conditions. A 'standard' brick wall is described as being one brick thick but that is in fact the length of the brick and not, as might be supposed, the width. A standard brick was, in the 19th century, 4in (101mm) by 9in (228mm) and we must allow a little extra for the mortar joints which were thinner then than they are now. Modern bricks are not much smaller but are still laid with four courses to 1ft (305mm) in height which can be useful if estimating from photographs.

Mortar is weaker than the bricks themselves and so to ensure that the wall did not fall apart the bricks were laid in 'bond' so that some bricks were laid sideways while others were laid across the wall. Different systems were used for different purposes and in different areas so it is best to study the building you are trying to re-create. In English bond one row of bricks is laid with all the bricks lengthways and the next row is laid with them all crossways. In Flemish bond one is laid

Stretcher bond, seen on most new houses where the outer leaf of the wall is only a single thickness with no bricks going through to the inner leaf.

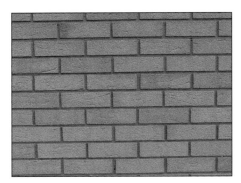

Flemish bond, Acle, Norfolk.

English bond, Feltwell, Norfolk.

An unusual bond often used on barns for cheapness where a mix of bricks and local flint make up the outer skin of the wall.

Look out for brick details such as plinths, shown here, and the way door and window frames are set back into walls. Weybourne, North Norfolk Railway.

A typical 'spandrel' in cast iron at Weybourne. Commercial etchings are available but if your railway featured company initials then it may be possible to persuade an etched kit manufacturer to produce them as specials. The M&GN spandrels shown on the model of Cromer Beach came via this route.

sideways and the next lengthways in every course. In a 'garden wall bond' one row is laid endways and then five rows laid sideways. The most common bond used nowadays is 'stretcher bond' in which every row is laid lengthways as there is a cavity between the outer and inner leaves of brickwork so no bricks are laid right through the wall. The strength of the double thickness wall is gained by linking the two leaves by steel ties.

Materials for walls

Your choice of material for walls depends a great deal on the size of the wall. Card is great in the smaller scales but for O gauge and larger you will need ply, MDF or a foam board. Foam board is very easy to shape but can be dissolved by some solvents if you are adding styrene details.

Commercial brick and stone papers are available from several sources and provide a quick and effective means of producing walls. Cut out the window openings and take the paper round them, then stick to the back of the wall. Think carefully about placing your paper to go round the main corners too. If you need a join then try to arrange it where it will be concealed by a rainwater pipe or a tree.

If you are going to use the face of card by scribing the detail then the card should be thick enough to resist bowing, probably 1mm thick for 2mm scale and possibly 4mm scale, but 2mm for 7mm scale and above. All card buildings need bracing to keep them square and this can usually be arranged as the floors. Cutting floors exactly the right size can be a pain

Above: Brickpapers from Superquick.

A quick terrace at the back of the railway, constructed from brickpaper and Alphagraphix doors and windows. As it is normally only seen head-on the lack of texture doesn't matter. The fence was drawn and photocopied onto tracing paper. Below the houses runs a half-hidden track on its way to the fiddle yard.

The basic card structure for buildings using embossed plastic or brickpaper.

Top left: A basic window aperture ready for detailing.

Top centre: The brick paper has been glued on and tucked round the corners.

Top right: The rear face of the window.

Above left: The arch detail has been cut from a block of bricks, individual bricks sliced along the mortar joints and teased apart.

Above centre The arch detail has been glued on and adds some texture.

so cut them smaller and stick right angled triangles of card just underneath or above to fix them in place. If you need strength then it is possible to build up a laminate of several layers of card using PVA glue. This works well for bridges and curved structures. Consider at an early stage how you will make your building look permanent and not just stuck onto the surface of the ground. You can bed it in with your grass, road or platform material but this usually means sticking it down, making it difficult to remove for repairs or if you need to remove it from a portable layout. The usually accepted method for making the building look as if it has grown out of the ground is to take the walls down into the surface. You carefully cut a hole in your ground and sink the building in. Tufts of grass or gravel taken right to the wall edge add to the effect.

You will need to provide surface detail such as bricks or stone for the walls. This may be in flat or embossed brickpaper, eg Howard Scenics, or embossed plastic eg Slaters. This is very much a matter of 'horses for courses' and you need to choose appropriately if you have arches or stone 'quoins' which need to be wrapped round into window openings. Arches can be made from individual bricks cut from the sheet or from strips of bricks sliced almost through and distorted to shape. Gaps can be filled in DAS or Milliput putty. Howard Scenics sheets come with pre-formed arches which make the job easier as do some of the flat brick paper sheets, eg Superquick. These look fine when viewed head-on but are not realistic when seen from an angle.

Above right: Using the soldering iron to shape the brick arches for a viaduct using a small plate as a radius template.

I am impatient and so when I needed lots of angled bricks in the arches of a viaduct I used a soldering iron with the bit filed to screwdriver shape to melt them into shape.

Attaching embossed brick sheets to a card or MDF structure is a bit of an art. Styrene doesn't like sticking to PVA and superglue is rather expensive so my personal solution is to use Evo Stik. Spread it evenly over both brick and wall base then leave to dry for about 10 minutes. Carefully align the sheet where you want it to be and press down hard. You need to make sure it is all in contact with the base or you will leave a void which fills with evaporating solvent that eventually softens the outer skin causing it to warp. Buildings should not be completely sealed so as to avoid a build-up of solvent inside. Leave a window open. Evo Stik can eat foam board with a vengeance so either leave it to evaporate for several minutes or try something more gentle like Copydex, though you will have to work harder to get the plastic to make good contact.

Some modellers prefer to work entirely in plastic sheet. This signalbox is modelled on the one at Cromer Beach and will be completed as it is today to accompany an up to date model. My own Cromer Beach 'box was built in similar fashion but as it was in the 1930s. Photo and model: Chris Turnbull

This country station building uses plastic brick sheet to create details such as the corbelling (brick pattern under the edge of the roof), brick arches and windows. The paper roof slates are described later. The corrugated iron roof is a Christmas decoration saved in the scrap box since 1970 but can be bought commercially.

Signalboxes really lend themselves to construction in card and plastic. This delightful model is the work of Nigel Digby.

Colouring embossed plastic or card sheets can be achieved in several different ways and the choice is probably more to do with personal confidence and preference than anything. You can paint the whole thing with mortar colour (remember to include some variation) and then add the masonry colour afterwards or you can run or rub in the cement pointing after the main colour. Some people like to add colour to bricks using almost dry paint on a stiff brush. True dry brushing involves using pigments or weathering powders completely dry ands works well with embossed card. You can emboss your own card with a stylus held in a kind of chuck (available from art shops) or I use a 9H pencil kept sharp which also adds mortar colour. This is a bit too grey, especially for older mortars which were made with lime and had a creamier colour. Being of a lazy nature I sometimes apply my main brick colour using a small rubber roller (try the art shops again). Mix the paint on a smooth biscuit tin lid but don't mix too well; then you get automatic variation in colour. Roll over the paint and spread it out, then test on scrap material until it just sticks to the raised detail. This technique is very satisfying when it works well. It needs little touching up afterwards. Remember to touch up afterwards where you have cut into the base plastic to form window openings etc.

The stages in creating walls and windows in card

A good quality card is required for scribing and then your chosen tool will create the indentations without tearing. The best tools are a pointed stylus with a rounded tip such as used to be sold for hand drawing on Gestetner stencils or (my preference) a hard pencil (4H — 9H). The pencil can be sharpened to a fine point and can be applied quite firmly to the surface of the card to produce the relief of bricks or flat-faced stone/

For stone walls using a pencil gives the advantage of some colour to the mortar course and has a familiar feel to the user.

First stage is to mark out the side of the building including the window apertures. Next comes the scribing of the horizontal lines.

Speeding things up a bit, using embossed plastic sheet

Plastic brick sheets by Slaters and embossed brick papers such as those by Howard Scenics give more regular representations of bricks for ordinary folk like me. They still need to be coloured but the technique is slightly different. Everyone has their

A basic 1mm thick card wall for a 4mm scale barn with timber frame and bricks scribed and watercoloured. The roof is to be thatched and for some reason I decided to build all the rafters and battens instead of just using a card roof.

Below left: 4mm scale walls scribed onto card and painted with watercolour. The ground floor wall is built in flint while the first floor is brick. The thatched roof is discussed later.

Below centre: The card side of the building with horizontal lines scribed.

Below: The vertical joints have been added — look closely at your subject to check the pattern or bond.

Above: The basic brick colour has been added by placing dabs of watercolour on a margarine pot lid and transferring by dabbing with a fingertip. Don't forget to scribe round corners into reveals and colour these too.

Above centre: Further watercolour is added to individual bricks, glazing (clear styrene) is stuck behind the wall with Evo Stik and then glazing bars added from styrene 'microstrip'. The trick here is to apply solvent to the microstrip only and position carefully before slicing off the end with the knife point.

Above right: A brush over with grey/brown weathering powder to fill the mortar joints and the window is complete.

own preferences but I like to start with creamy grey wash to colour the mortar courses. Others prefer to wash these in after painting the main brick colour. Acrylic paint is best for this as it can be wiped off before drying onto the main bricks, leaving the mortar courses to hold the colour. My next stage involves using a small roller as sold for lino printing (remind me to talk about lino later when we consider bridges).

I have a stiff tin lid onto which I pour several slightly different shades of brick colour paint which are then spread out by the roller (but not too well mixed as this gives the mottling effect typical of older brickwork). As mentioned earlier my favourite colour for light red bricks is, oddly enough, London & South Western coach salmon (good for flesh too). Bricks from the West Midlands need more of a rust colour while engineer's blue bricks need a touch of blue tending towards purple. Compare results in the same light with a colour photo of what you are trying to achieve. As with card you will need to highlight some bricks in different shades and colour in some that the roller misses. Other techniques to try are using a fine sponge to apply the paint and of course the good old fingertips!

Attaching the brick to the basic structure

Whether your main structure is made of card, ply or foam board the technique is the same. Cut the brick sides oversize and feather the edges to make a good joint.

Banningham New Mill, based on a building in Wisbech, Cambs, has all English bond brick scribed on card — satisfying but soul-destroying. However, there is help at hand in the shape of embossed paper and plastic sheets.

Stick the plastic to the structure with Evo Stik, coating both surfaces (somebody please come up with a less messy way) and work fairly quickly so that most of the solvent has evaporated so as not to stay in place to warp the sheets but still fluid enough to be able to press down hard for good contact. I then cut out the window openings but leave some plastic to go into the openings (reveals). To get a good sharp bend you need to scribe the inside of the sheet adjacent to the edge of the opening to create a groove. I use a very fine knife blade for this. You may find that you end up cutting right through but this doesn't matter as you can re-make the joint afterwards. A little more Evo Stik and pressure with fingers allows you to make a tight joint. Some trimming may be necessary at the back.

Stone walls

There are many different ways to create stone walls and your choice will depend on the type of stone being modelled and your personal abilities.

The kind of patterns used for building in stone depend on the purpose of the wall (dry stone walls round fields or finely faced stone for cathedrals, with fairly good quality work for station buildings and a more random sort for bridges etc) and on the type of stone available.

Fine quality dressed stone, usually limestone, would be transported many miles for the construction of expensive buildings such as cathedrals. In the Middle Ages

*Below: The structure
has been assembled
and the first wall of
brick attached. The
reveals have been
scribed from the rear
and folded round. Note
the wall is oversized
and feather edged.*

*Botton left: The
completed platelayers'
hut.*

*Bottom: This detail
from Fitton End station
shows corbelling, brick
arch scribed into the
plastic sheet, reveals
and the window made
from microstrip.*

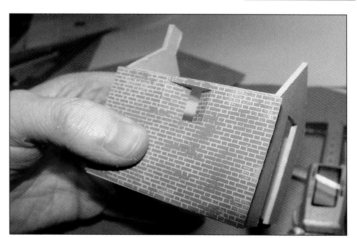

stone was imported from France (Caen stone) for building churches and to a lesser extent Portland stone would be moved around the country. These stones would be cut into rectangular blocks and laid in the same way as bricks.

Sandstones and courser limestones could also be cut into blocks but were frequently left rough on the front. For lesser quality walls these would be laid in the shapes as they came out of the quarry. They were generally laid in courses, though the courses were broken at times. The builders would never build with long vertical joints as this would weaken the wall. Many of the older, harder rocks found in Cornwall, Wales, the Lake District and Scotland were laid in rough courses as it took a lot of effort to break these into small blocks. Look out for local variations such as the unusual Carrstone walling of Norfolk (very small flat pieces of ironstone). Soft chalk is sometimes seen in blocks in cottages but never used for railway buildings. Flint, a very hard round or knobbly stone found in chalk, is common throughout the southeast of England. This is laid in approximate courses or sometimes cut (knapped) into more regular square blocks. Most of the softer stones have corners (quoins) made of a harder stone or brick. Some stonework has small hard stones pushed into the mortar to protect it. This process is called 'galleting' and is easy to reproduce on scribed walling such as chalk by using a fine tipped pen.

And so to create these stone walls…

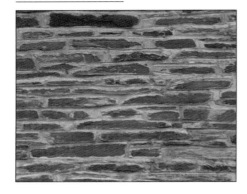

Right: The first stage is to paint your base with a coat of PVA glue. Before it sets fully spread on modelling clay (my favourite is DAS). Use a wooden coffee stirrer to make your own tool for pressing V shaped joints between the stones. Stonework is also bonded (ie no long continuous vertical joints) and various styles use either uniform-sized blocks or a mix of sizes. Our demonstration panel uses a mix and we are going to attempt to imitate the millstone grit walling found in the Pennines.

Above right: Gentle brushing with a hogs' hair brush and adjustments with a small knife blade smooth out the outlines of the stones. The same knife blade can produce some of the grain in the stones.

Right: Next, on with your base colour. For millstone grit ochre or matt earth enamel seems to work best. Pick out individual stones in slightly different shades and shake some talc on for a super matt effect.

Above right: Finally a brush with weathering powders to simulate soot in the pointing and any hollows.

Yes, you can use papers which are very effective from a distance, especially the Faller ones or embossed plastic sheets. These can be used in much the same way as embossed brick sheets, cutting individual stones to suit at corners and reveals. Painting is the key to effective use of them and the best method seems to be to paint a mottled base coat in (usually) a grey colour and then pick out highlights with several different shades using dry brushing. Either use a very stiff brush with enamels or acrylic paint almost dry or the same stiff brush with weathering powders. You can fix the final effect with a matt varnish. Ronseal works and can be sprayed with an airbrush or you can invest in Testors Dullcote. I also sometimes blow talc onto wet paint to add to the matt effect.

If you need to create stonework with lots of relief then modelling clay can give it real depth. It takes a while but is quite therapeutic.

Individual stone walls to any style can be built up using modelling clay (eg DAS) or even plasticene. Artists' acrylic paint can be used for this process, but is expensive. The technique involves spreading your clay over the sub structure (ply

Below left: Limestone buildings and those in the countryside tend to be lighter as in this example built by Mark Knowles and John Walker-Smith.

Below: This house is based on a typical Edwardian example with flint pebble walls. These are formed from Slaters plastic sheets with plastic brick quoins. It is in low relief against the backscene but blended in using vegetation.

Above: The 19th century saw much use of corrugated iron both for railway buildings and for buildings such as this chapel, built by Bill Davis. Corrugated iron sheets are available from Wills for 4mm scale and Duncan Models for 7mm scale.

or card), usually after applying a bonding coat of PVA glue. Don't apply too much at once or it will dry before you finish. You can then form the individual stones and courses with modelling tools and even a pencil. DAS usually comes in grey or you can mix your base colour in acrylic then paint as for the plastic sheets described above.

Dry stone walls are constructed of stones cleared from the fields. They were mostly constructed during a relatively short period in history during the enclosures which pre-dated the railways. These can be obtained as resin or plaster castings which are quite effective if some care is taken with the joints. I once built quite a lot of these for 4mm scale using chippings left over from resurfacing the road.

Windows

The style of windows in a building is often one of the main features which give it its character. The use of classical-styled windows in modern housing gives an older feel to some developments. We may occasionally see very early styles of window in buildings near the railway but usually the Victorian sliding sash is seen in quantities.

Multiple bar Georgian-style windows were seen on some station buildings and enjoyed a revival on public buildings in the 1950s.

Creating your windows

Here's another area where there are as many different methods as there are modellers. Without doubt the best windows available are the etched ones from GT Models or resin ones from Port Wynnstay, but there are some quite acceptable ones printed on plastic sheet. Even windows printed on paper or card can look right provided they are recessed into the building. You can make your own by drawing them at an enlarged scale and reducing them on a photocopier to your chosen scale. In the past I made some by using a bow pen and white enamel onto styrene sheet by tracing over a drawing of the building. These did have a little relief but were not as effective as making them from strips of styrene sheet fixed to plastiglaze with solvent. To do this effectively you need to wet the strip with solvent, then stick it

Window styles.

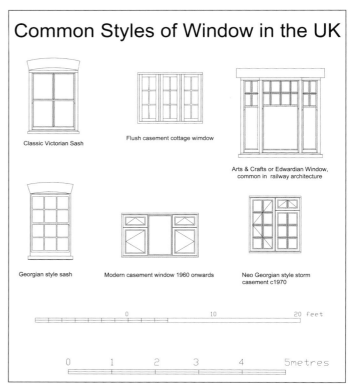

Common Styles of Window in the UK

Classic Victorian Sash

Flush casement cottage wimdow

Arts & Crafts or Edwardian Window, common in railway architecture

Georgian style sash

Modern casement window 1960 onwards

Neo Georgian style storm casement c1970

0   10   20 feet

0   1   2   3   4   5metres

onto the plastiglaze over your building drawing without allowing any sideways slide which will show on the bits you need to keep clear.

You can build up any design of window using this technique and, as usual, study the real thing or photographs to get the depths and profiles right. Windows of older railway buildings and domestic houses were usually set back at least 3in (75mm) behind the face of the brickwork.

Roofs

Roofs are not usually seen from the ground but are so obvious from the air, which is the normal viewing angle for our layouts. For this reason we need to pay particular attention to the details and texture of them. Chimneys look small from the ground but are usually bigger than we think. The technique of counting bricks is really useful here if we are to get the proportions right. Chimney pots are huge (have you ever seen one on the ground?) and repay attention to detail. A typical size is around 9in (225mm) across, so at least start with a tube of that size and if you want to get really accurate then try turning them. (Use your electric drill if you don't have a lathe.) Chimneys have various details such as two rows of bricks corbelled out at the top and usually the pots are bedded in concrete (flaunching) best simulated in DAS or Milliput. I have yet to see a smoke unit fitted, but then most layouts seem to be set in midsummer don't they?

Using microstrip to complete the window made earlier. The technique I prefer is to wet one side of the strip with solvent using a brush, stick one end down carefully and then trim in situ with my favourite XActo offset blade in a No1 knife. Others will prefer the Swann Morton scalpel but I like to be able to rotate the blade with a pencil-like action.

Resin window frames by Port Wynnstay.

Printed window frames by Superquick.

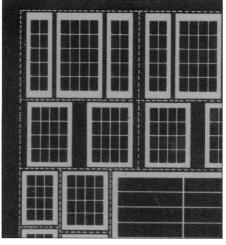

The completed station building at Cromer Beach. Fortunately, most of the fine timber mouldings for windows are white, the same as microstrip! The awning is in plastic sheet, the columns are castings and the spandrels were a specially commissioned etch. The tiles took a week in front of the television.

Our platelayers' hut has been temporarily 'planted' on some Green Scene meadow grass mat. A turned aluminium chimney pot has been added, flaunched with Milliput 'cement', the slates painted and some moss and lichen has grown on the roof. A few weeds round the base from Woodland Scenics foam help to conceal the join between building and ground. Notice how some slates have been 'distressed' and dislodged.

I mentioned texture above and this is so easy to achieve. In real life slates and tiles are fixed individually to battens nailed to the rafters (the main structural members) of the roof. For our models we can use strips of paper or card to represent lines of tiles. My favourite method is to use paper of an appropriate thickness from books purchased at charity shops. First you need to find out the thickness of your real life slate or tile. Let's say you have a 15mm thick tile (go and measure some in the builders' merchants). Work out how thick 10 of them would be in your chosen scale. For 4mm scale ten 15mm thick tiles would be 10 x 15 divided by 76 = just under 2mm. Now go round the charity shops and look for books with paper that gives 10 pages at 2mm thick (take your digital calipers, at £9.99 from Aldi if you like).

Take your chosen book home and fold over the pages. Mark out the horizontal spacing between slates and score deeply. Cut off strips of slates and stick them to the roof, distressing and breaking a few on the way. I prefer Evo Stik for this operation but experiment with your favourite glues. Paint with a base colour then highlight individual slates/tiles as appropriate. Ridge tiles for slate roofs have an angular top and can be made from strips of styrene but clay ridges for tiles are usually semi-circular and I find the best material is the insulation stripped from electric cable. Score it to give the lines between individual ridge tiles.

Unusual tiles such as pantiles, common in Somerset, East Anglia and East Yorkshire need a different approach. Wills and Slaters provide embossed sheets

Cutting slates or tiles using the folded book method. Each stroke of the knife cuts many pages of the book. Strips of tiles are then cut off to be stuck onto the roof.

Sticking on the strips of slates to the platelayers' hut.

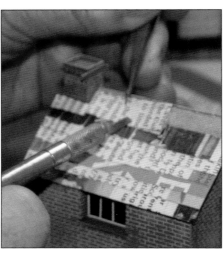

Noch embossed pantiles.

Cotswold stone slates, Aynho, Northants.

for these which are acceptable from a distance but don't quite have the required relief, while Noch have an embossed sheet which is better if not quite accurate for 7mm scale. 2mm and 3mm scales are not well catered for here. Slaters have 2mm scale brick but the limitations of the embossing process make the bricks a little 'knobbly' for my liking. I have created pantiles by covering the roof with plasticene and then pressing a forming tool made of brass into the plasticene at regular intervals to give the relief of the tiles. This is fine for old buildings where the roof is uneven but not so good if you want a more regular effect.

Until the coming of the railways roofing materials, like those used for walls, were not transported far. Slates were unheard of outside of the areas where they were quarried — Wales, the Lake District and Cornwall. Thicker stone slates could be found wherever there were suitable layers of sandstone or limestone to make them from — mainly Dorset, the Cotswolds and the Pennines.

Corrugated iron roofs are common on railway buildings and it is possible to buy suitable sections for this. I am still using some foil Christmas decorations from the 1960s which were perfect for 7mm scale roofs!

Thatch is probably the most difficult roofing material to create convincingly. My first visit to Pendon Museum started me on using human hair. Roye England's original technique involved sort of sewing the hair onto the card roof. One of his early assistants started using plumber's hemp but sticking it down. This was more effective and Roye's early buildings were improved by this technique. I stayed with hair as I found a convenient supply at the local ladies' hairdressers but I stuck it down. My technique involves placing a layer of PVA glue on the card roof and then

Detail of the gable of the cottage, showing brick with flint panels, tile hanging and such neat thatch. If we made our model thatch that smooth it would not look right!

This pair of thatched cottages from Wherwell in Hampshire had traditional vegetable gardens when I visited in 1968. The cabbages are peppercorns and the pile of firewood comes from heather stalks as does the tree in the front garden. The apple and plum trees are from twisted wire. The neatly trimmed hedges are of foam rubber and the pump was soldered from offcuts of metal tube. Note the washing on the line.

getting a bunch of hair about 25mm long and dipping one end into polycell wallpaper adhesive. Initially stick this down onto the PVA layer then gently flatten it. This gives the correct angle but is uneven. Repeat the process up the roof until you reach the ridge. The polycell moves through the fibres by capillary action and the roof at this point looks a mess. You will have used a year's supply of adrenalin worrying about what the final result looks like. Put it away for 24 hours or more, then when it is dry start to trim with a brand new razor blade. (If you can't get single edged ones cover one side with several layers of masking tape to protect fingers.) Do the other side of the roof and repeat the trimming then start on the ridge. This is made by laying two lines of PVA glue on a sheet of polythene. Carefully lay bunches of hair over them and 'puddle' the hair into the PVA so it sticks. When dry you should have two rigid lines which can be trimmed with the razor blade to make fancy patterns and a flexible middle section. Stick one side to one side of the roof with PVA or Evo Stik and leave to dry for a day. Next day you will need to force the middle section to bend over onto the glue for the other side of the roof. Pin it down or even sew on the hazel rods that the thatcher would use and then leave to set.

The best colour for the base coat of paint is matt earth but you can experiment depending on the colour of hair used (blonde for new thatch will need little colouring but will need matt varnish as it will otherwise shine). Older thatch will need patches of moss painting on or, if really getting past its best, try patches of Woodland Scenics foam foliage to simulate moss.

Another view of 34 Winchester Road with the White Lion in the background. Note the pump outside the front door.

Commissioned buildings

I have left this option until last as it needs careful consideration and a visit to the bank manager. There are just a few suppliers out there who can produce buildings to match the quality of the best locomotives and coaches available. But you wouldn't expect them to spend as long creating your building as a locomotive builder would spend on your locomotive and then charge next to nothing would you? I have used this option just once in the case of a signalbox which I asked Nigel Digby to build as he had already built one in another scale and knew the building. The signalbox is illustrated earlier in this chapter. It was a wise decision as I think you will agree. Geoff Taylor produced the Homfirth buildings, while another supplier of model buildings to commission is Kirtley Model Buildings, generally O gauge and above.

I took this picture in Holmfirth with a view to making a model but then saw I had been beaten to it by one of the masters.

For super realism try these, transplanted a few miles to Manchester Model Railway Society's 'Dewsbury Midland' layout by Geoff Taylor. Manchester Model Railway Society

Bridges, structures and furniture

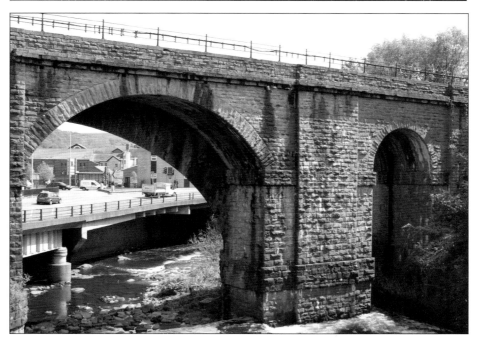

The viaduct at Pontypridd (Taff Vale Railway) would challenge any modeller as it features arches of different shapes and is set on a wye-junction where lines going north diverge.

Railways need gentle gradients and wide curves and these needs mean that the construction of a railway disturbs the landscape much more than a road does. Wherever the railway crosses a road or river some form of structure is needed. Even level crossings need gates.

Except in flat countryside the railway is often routed a little above a valley bottom as the valley provides the easiest route without tunnels or deep cuttings and the railway is less likely to flood. This means that bridges are needed over rivers and often over roads and other railways.

Many early bridges were simple single semi-circular arches in brick or stone but soon the railway engineers devised more complex solutions to difficult situations. Before embarking on such elaborate works as the Saltash Bridge, Brunel was a pioneer of the long elliptical span. His critics were convinced that the bridge over the Thames at Maidenhead would not stand up, let alone carry heavy modern trains 180 years later at well over 100mph. These bridges are fairly easy to construct in embossed brick or stone, the difficult part being the creation of the

A slightly simpler but still interesting viaduct can be found north of Alston in Cumbria.

A much less complicated and very common type of bridge, typical of many railways. This accommodation underbridge in brick is at Wherwell, LSWR.

Above: This bridge, based on Ledbury Viaduct and built by Sandy Croall, is a scene in itself. See Chapter 10 for ideas on self-contained scenes.

Above right 'Fitton End Bridge' is a mongrel, having some elements of design from the M&GN and some from the GER but is typical of a plate girder bridge. The water is layers of PVA and varnish.

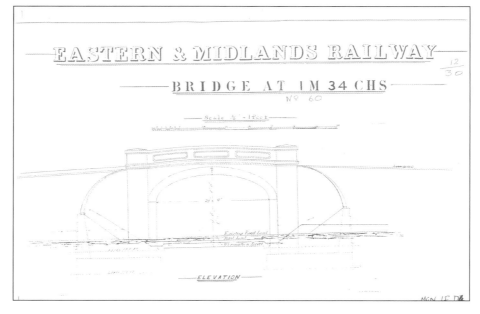

EASTERN & MIDLANDS RAILWAY

BRIDGE AT 1M 34 CHS

Nº 60

ELEVATION

Above left: A typical brick-arched bridge from the mid- to late-19th century.

Left: Detail of the plate girder bridge at Trehafod, Taff Vale Railway. This may be a later Great Western Railway replacement.

Preserved railways are a useful source of inspiration and photographs. The overbridge at Quorn on the Great Central Railway is a steel joists bridge with brick abutments and parapet walls.

rows of brick that form the arches. These can be made up of strips of brick cut from the sheet and curved round or can be melted in as seen in Chapter 4. Some brick papers and the Howard Scenics sheets have arches ready printed and these can be a time saver. Peco and Langley supply some useful generic arched bridges which can be used as they are or modified to suit some railways.

Victorian engineers soon took the iron bridge concept and developed it into a highly complex technology and art form. Indeed, many of the surviving structures such as the Saltash and Forth Bridges are regarded as national monuments. Many others are listed structures, legally preserved and requiring special permission before alterations can be carried out.

Plate girder bridges are probably the most common steel structures on our railways and these can be relatively easy to construct from plastic sheet or metal.

The more intricate structures seen in lattice girder bridges can also be constructed using plastic components, especially if compromise allows the use of 'almost correct' components from Plastruct or others. If there is no alternative but complete scratchbuilding, then the prefabricated approach is likely to be the best option. For this you can set up jigs by fixing strips of aluminium or pins onto a solid base. The components can then be soldered together from brass strip or angle, or can be solvent-welded in the case of plastic parts. If using plastic then polythene is the best material to lay over the base as solvents do not easily stick to it.

Richard Turner has modelled this bridge on Charwelton in the Great Central style.

The swing bridge at Sutton Bridge on the M&GN originally had rails on one side and road on the other. Built in 1897, it is still in use today carrying the A17 trunk road. This model, built in 2mm:ft scale by Reg Cooper and Richard Stowe, captures the prototype very well.

Each railway had its own design of bridge but the economics of kit production mean that very few accurate bridges are available to suit a particular location. The Peco girder bridge provides an effective generic example which may be customised to a certain extent.

Footbridges are rarely modelled accurately, due to their infinite variety and delicate structure. The Airfix (now Dapol) footbridge kit graced many a 4mm scale station in the 1960s but was a very bland interpretation of a generic

style of footbridge and was used more as a symbolic bridge than an attempt at accurate representation of a particular structure.

The advent of the Ratio footbridge provided a better representation of a covered bridge and, if you are fortunate enough to model in 7mm scale, the Loveless GWR footbridge gives a superb, if expensive, basis for a very accurate GWR bridge.

Tunnel mouths are another distinctive feature which were usually plain and functional but occasionally, as at Box in Wiltshire and on the Great Eastern Railway line to Cambridge, could be quite decorative. The simplest tunnel mouth is a flat brick or stone wall with an arch; however, the shape of the arch varies a great deal even between examples on the same railway. Some have vertical sides with a semi-circular arch, others are formed of circular arches with the trackbed in a chord at the base while others, such as some on the London, Brighton & South Coast Railway, are a tall ellipse. The design of the tunnel mouth can sometimes reflect the conditions found when the tunnel was built and the methods used to hold back the pressure from the rocks above. In solid rock no lining is necessary but in clays, sands and chalk several layers of brick are needed to stop collapse.

Commercially available tunnel mouths include those by Peco and Gaugemaster, both economical and effective. It has been claimed that the Peco tunnel mouth is incorrect in that it has abutment walls but in fact these were quite common on some railways. The Gaugemaster examples exhibit a different style while if you are prepared to pay a little more those by Bradnor Branchline are based on actual prototypes. Commercial offerings for O gauge are even more limited but there are the very realistic stone ones from Enhance Ecosse, marketed by Skytrex.

The textured mouldings of the Enhance Ecosse tunnel mouth from Skytrex makes a most effective sandstone example as seen throughout the Midlands and North West.

The green green grass

A typical country lane in summer, full of light feathery foliage of cow parsley at Crimplesham, Norfolk.

M odellers of the urban or industrial scenes may be thinking of skipping this chapter — but first look at a couple of prototype examples and see if you find vegetation such as brambles, buddleia bushes or even small trees growing in the gutters.

Foliage, hedges and fences, grass and other plants

The fact is, we are surrounded by plants and they will find a place to grow if we leave land and buildings untended for any length of time. A disused railway yard in Cambridge looks like a forest of birch trees after 10 years without maintenance, while our railway embankments, which were neatly cut by hand in the first hundred years of railways, became a forest of sycamore trees producing quantities of 'the wrong kind of leaves' causing delays to commuters. In recent years, since 1995 a major tree cutting programme has opened up many railway earthworks to something more like their previous form.

Some of the greatest modellers have managed to produce layouts on which the scenery has been minimal, the grass represented only by smooth areas of pale colour and yet serving admirably as a background to the trains. The late W. S. Norris provided very effective simple scenery for his railway with little or no texture and the key to its effectiveness lay in its simplicity. There were no distractions and the eye was led to the trains or to the equally simple background. Later modellers started to add texture in the form of dyed sawdust and then the revolution started. In the early 1960s a material called flock started to be marketed, championed by the editor of the *Model Railway Constructor*. Once a modeller had used this there was no going back to sawdust. This is still the most popular way of portraying grass and has advanced a long way since those early days. Techniques for applying flock are discussed in detail later in this chapter.

Grass is the most common vegetation found alongside railway lines and is well represented by any thin fibre which can simulate the tall thin strands of most grass plants. The flock mentioned above can be purchased already attached to a foliage mat and provides a very quick way to create large areas of textured scene.

However, smooth, even grass of uniform size is restricted to lawns and golf courses. Railway earthworks and most farm fields feature grass of varying lengths and also include a variety of other plants. Even in the closely grazed grass fields on a dairy farm there will be clumps of higher grass of a richer green colour where the animals have deposited 'cowpats'. Most other fields will have 'weeds' such as docks and nettles while in areas where weedkiller is only lightly used on adjacent arable fields there will be buttercups and daisies in their season. On less-well-tended land such as beside the railway there will be brambles, particularly if the model is set from the 1960s onwards when routine cutting of the railway banks was discontinued.

Creations of realistic representations of these mixed types of foliage requires the modeller to have an armoury of materials and techniques to show the variety noted above. Flock powders by Noch, Heki and others need to be supplemented by materials such as minced foam clumps by Woodland Scenics, Javis, Green Scene or Hornby and by foliage nets such as Woodland Scenics. These nets make excellent brambles and are very useful in making some kinds of trees as we shall see in the next chapter. A little piece of foliage net draped against a fence post makes a good representation of the sort of bushes found along railway boundaries and can often serve to conceal places such as where fences are interrupted at baseboard joints.

The key to getting these materials to form a realistic scene lies in the way they are attached to the baseboard. PVA glue is the commonly accepted standard method of attaching basic foliage to the baseboard but is supplemented by Spray Mount or even hairspray where a secondary layer is to be added. The PVA glue method tends to leave the grass more or less horizontal, fine for mown areas but not quite like the vertical growth of lush long grass. For many years I resorted to planting individual small clusters of foliage vertically, a very time-consuming process, but now there is help at hand in the form of the Noch Grassmaster and the Green Scene equivalent. These devices impart a static charge to the fibres which cause them to leave the container vertically when it is gently shaken. It is possible to achieve the same effect using balloons or a comb rubbed with nylon to give a charge but this is very hit and miss when compared with the commercial devices above. The Noch puffer bottle gives a slightly less dramatic effect for less cost but takes a long time to apply the product.

Grass tufts from Mini Natur bring extra realism to this summer scene. Yellow ragwort flowers come from the same stable and the foxgloves came from a tree in my neighbour's garden, sprayed over with red acrylic car paint.

Applying PVA glue to a large area needs care if it is not to 'skin' and prevent adhesion. First spray the area with water, especially if the base is card or plaster which will soak up the glue rather quickly. Dilute the PVA with about a third water to help it flow, not too much or it will run down slopes, then apply with a one-inch brush. As you move over a large area spray the early parts with water to keep the glue fresh. Scatter or puff your flock in patches of slightly different colours and add a little minced foam (possibly with some red or yellow flowers) but don't go right to the edge of your glued area until you have applied the next section of glue.

Study prototype pictures of the kind of foliage you are creating to find out if there are plants such as rushes, common in damp fields and on moorlands, or nettles, which are taller and darker than most grass. Clumps or tufts of longer grass can be added from the International Models range or you can make your own. Buy a pack of long fibres (International Models) and pull clumps between your finger ends. Keep pinching one end and dip it into PVA glue. Stick down in the field or onto polythene sheet. You can lift from the polythene sheet when dry to use anywhere.

Rough or dead autumn grass can be represented by fur fabric. To save you searching, Green Scene have sourced an appropriate grade which just requires a little touching up with shades of green as completely dead grass is rare in the UK. For even rougher grass or reedbeds goat hair as sold by specialist builders' merchants for reinforcing plaster is ideal. This can be dyed or sprayed for different effects.

Many other fibres have been used to represent grass. Moorland and rough grass scenes can be created with the fibre used to line hanging baskets or with dyed lint cloth. The technique with lint is to dye it then stick it down to the baseboard with PVA. Once set it has to be ripped off quite forcefully, leaving much of the fibre sticking up. It requires a secondary treatment with other slightly different shades of loose fibre or foam to take away the uniformity which comes with using all one shade.

Using the Noch Grassmaster, shaking gently to allow the statically charged grass to slip out the right way up.

Centre left: The resulting grass after hoovering up the surplus.

Below: Rough grass from Green Scene, also known as fur fabric. The rough grass can be 'cut' using a hot-air gun, the heat shrinking the fibres. However, beware of the surrounding area, and fingers, when applying heat!

Below left: Even rougher grass from dyed goat hair.

Below: Home made grass tufts on a polythene bag.

Bushes have been mentioned above and several different varieties can be created using clump foliage and foliage net, depending on the density of foliage required. Flowering bushes need careful application of small pieces of coloured foam or even tiny pieces of paper. Garden flowers are sold by Busch but are expensive if you require large quantities. As supplied they are very bright, in fact just as bright as the real thing but they seem a little too brash and toy-like if left like that. A wash or spray with a wash of very dilute 'mud'-coloured acrylic paint tones them down just enough. Busch also make some lovely ferns which need painting with dull green acrylic paint (golden brown for an autumn scene). Acrylic paint seems to give just the right amount of sheen for natural-looking foliage. ER Decor (from the Model Landscape Company, Potter Heigham, Norfolk) produce a very realistic range of garden plants and accessories from laser cut photographs and these appear about the right brightness.

A characteristic plant of untended land is the rosebay willow herb, a plant which grows to about 3ft (915mm) tall and has pink flowers from June onwards and wispy flying seeds in September. To create these in flower try strands of dyed goat hair with the usual spray mount or hairspray coating and Green Scene dyed foam. I haven't tried the autumn variety but it might be achieved with the really pale dead grass mix from Green Scene. Other, partially managed land will grow tall plants with white flowers such as hogweed, cow parsley or kek. These can be simulated with tiny branches which break off your sea moss forests (see Chapter 7). A blob of white paint completes the flower. In more shaded lanes you will find foxgloves. A natural shrub which grows in my friend's garden and is also sold by Green Scene makes almost perfect foxgloves without further treatment but is best painted as the flowers will lose their colour over time.

There are several other 'special' kinds of foliage such as cornfields and farm crops (see Chapter 9) which need unusual techniques. Cornfields can be represented by the golden-coloured doormats made from coconut fibre. Place one piece at a low level to represent the stubble left behind after the crop has been harvested and another alongside it at a higher level to represent the uncut crop. Busch and ER Decor also sell materials for cornfields. Place a combine harvester or reaper and binder in the field and add the personnel carrying out the harvest.

Busch flowers are accurately moulded in self-coloured plastic. My eye suggests that they would look more natural with a little dull acrylic medium with a touch of grey washed over them.
.

These laser-cut plants are from ER decor in Belgium, imported by the Model Landscape company in Norfolk. The wooden sticks go by the name of 'Bonenstaken'.

This model country lane has its share of summer flowers but in hindsight I think I should have added more white flowers from Mini Natur to simulate the cow parsley.

More of my neighbour's tree foxgloves along with ferns from ER Decor and their grass tufts cling to the top of the Woodland Scenics rock mould. Only after I had added the foliage did I realise I had not weathered the rock and it was still as pulled from the mould.

Prior to the widespread use of selective weedkillers in the 1950s the crop would have been peppered with bright red poppies. Poppies started to re-appear in the late 1990s when the use of weedkiller was scaled down a little. Mushrooms would often grow in the stubble but might not show up on a small scale model. Mushrooms growing in pasture land would make an interesting diversion if the model is set in September or October, the time of year when moist mornings and evenings favour mushrooms fruiting in the wild.

Most farm crops can be simulated by rows of foam clusters on straight lines of PVA glue but one unusual crop, the hops used in brewing, grow up tall poles or wires. Fortunately Busch provide these for 4mm scale.

Reeds and bulrushes can be found in most slow flowing waters and lakes. I have yet to find a way of reproducing these in bulk but planting dyed goat hair a few strands at a time in neat PVA works for small quantities. The comb trick for static electricity seems to keep them upright while the glue sets. Field rushes are found in clusters in many fields where the ground gets waterlogged. These can be produced by dropping the dyed goat hair into blobs of PVA on a polythene bag. The PVA does not stick to polythene so the clusters can be uprooted and stuck into the PVA mix as the main grass is applied.

Foxgloves and willow herb are found in abundance along most rural railway lines.

Ivy leaves from the Little Leaf Company (actually birch bracts) are glued to fibres from ER Decor.

Boundaries

Field and property boundaries are sometimes formed of hedges and there are several methods of producing these. We need to consider the purpose of the boundary and the degree of maintenance it receives before choosing a method.

Garden hedges of privet or hawthorn are usually fairly well maintained and can be simulated by a strip of dyed foam rubber. This is fairly easy to cut to form the neat lines of a garden hedge. Hedges at the roadside or those intended to keep farm animals enclosed in their fields are more sturdy and receive only the maintenance necessary to enable them to fulfil their function. These are usually of hawthorn, occasionally of beech or hazel, and are rarely evergreen. Many of these hedges date from the time *c*1700-1800 when the common fields were enclosed and have acquired additional species since they were planted. Most 'enclosure' hedges were of thorn but holly, oak and field maple trees would find their way into them and were sometimes left as 'standard' trees, particularly in the Midlands.

As the trees in these hedges grew taller, gaps appeared in the lower portions through which stock could escape. This was remedied by 'laying' the hedge. This process involved cutting half way through each tall plant, laying it on its side and weaving it through a line of stakes driven into the ground. A 'rope' of hazel rods was spun between the tops of these stakes to retain the laid branches. The hedge then continued to grow and serve its function. The process is still widely practised in England, particularly in the Midlands, and examples can be seen alongside the M1 motorway in Leicestershire.

In the smaller scales, a line of lichen with either minced foam or foliage net can provide these hedges. Strips of sponge loofah are available from Green Scene for larger scales and these need just a little trimming and foliage net to create effective field boundaries. I have not attempted to model a laid hedge but I'm sure it can be done with twisted wire as described later in Chapter 9.

Laid hedges are common throughout the Midlands and many other areas.

Railway boundaries were usually fenced and each company had its own preferred style for this. Several early lines adopted substantial post and rail fences but as these were costly to provide and maintain, many companies substituted simpler types, the most common being the simple post and wire system, usually with five wires, often strung between old sleepers split in half. Barbed wire was not usually used for railway boundaries but became very common for field boundaries in the 1950s. I have yet to see a really effective system for creating this but the soldered wire method described by Roger Lycett-Smith in *Model Railway Journal* No 188 comes very close.

Post and rail fences are available from Peco and Slaters and unless your prototype calls for a particularly unusual style these will be effective. It is, however, most important that the fences are placed realistically in relation to the ground. The Peco fences use triangular section rails which may not exactly match your company's fencing but they are jointed in a way which allows the fence to flex enough to change its angle to go up hills. Slaters rails are rectangular and do not flex as easily but if you join the rails at the posts at any change in direction as is done in real life then these fences will be even more effective. Post and wire at its simplest can be made from wooden sleepers split in half with cotton threads stretched between them. My technique involves wrapping them round a post at the end of the run and then attaching with superglue at key intermediate positions.

Where stone is plentiful the field boundaries and occasionally railway boundaries can be formed with dry stone walls. These are available as castings but as they are straight and flat they are difficult to form to the contours of the hilly land in which they are usually found. The alternative is to build your own and this is not as difficult as you might think. Once again the first task is to study the walls found in your chosen modelling area. Most walls of this type (except some in Cornwall and Wales) have the stones laid horizontally and many have a row of vertical capping stones. It is possible to build them using real stones if you can find a source of small enough ones in the bags of gravel in your local garden centre. If you visit your chosen area and look in stream beds you may find a supply of stones already graded to size by the water. (However, do not remove these from a National Park area as it is illegal.) These stones will already be of the right type (ie limestone, sandstone, shale, slate or granite) but if you cannot find any try making your own with coloured plaster or modelling clay, eg DAS. Simply lay out a flat patch of clay and allow to dry. Break up carefully by cracking against a straight edge and then start to lay your stones, using Evo Stik instead of the gravity used to hold together the full size examples.

A highly unusual railway boundary can be found beside the Talyllyn Railway in Wales. This consists of vertical slabs of slate, bound together at the top by twisted wire. This would be essential if you model this railway and could probably be produced using strips of styrene sheet.

Gates can give a regional or company identity to your boundaries and there are so many variations on the simple five-barred gate that it would take another book to go through them all. Again, study the prototype and obtain measurements if possible before deciding whether to purchase ready made or build from

Above left: Resin stone walls are available from several manufacturers. They are perfect for quick, realistic walling on the level but can look uncomfortable at changes in level.

Centre left: Real stone walls are an answer if you have difficult terrain to fence. On the left the 'stones' are made by pouring out a thin layer of the same coloured plaster mix as used in the rock moulds and then breaking it up. On the right the wall is made from gravel gathered at the edge of a road in Wales! Both are stuck together with Evo Stik.

Left: This is a common scene in many hilly areas. The gateposts are stone. This kind of gate can also be used to frame a view into the scene beyond.

scratch. Styrene sheet is my preferred method for scratchbuilding wooden fences and gates but soldered construction is possible. Since the 1950s tubular steel gates have become the norm and can be soldered up from wire. In modern image modelling you will also need steel mesh fencing for which you may need to visit a dressmaker's shop for delicate woven fabric used in embroidery and hat making. This will also supply you with wire netting for your chicken run or pig pen.

Wrought iron fencing and gates have been a feature of railway premises since the early days and are available from Scale-Link and others in various scales. Although the real thing was almost always painted gloss black or the railway's own colours it is best on the model to use dull paint and if the prototype was black use a dark grey paint.

Water features

Modelling water has presented a challenge to modellers ever since the creation of scenery became popular. Early attempts used waved glass over a dark painted base but more recently modellers have experimented with the use of thick coats of varnish and even PVA glue. Don Annison, the creator of 'Bassenthwaite' used ripple coat Artex for the waves on his lake. This was then coloured with acrylics and given several coats of varnish.

The author has made a slow flowing river by building up layers of PVA glue onto a light brown base. This works well for slightly muddy water such as the River Nene shown in the picture of Sutton Bridge in Chapter 5 but not for deep clear rivers or pools.

If your model requires a feature where it is essential to see through the water, such as a waterfall or overflowing tap or container, then there are now products such as 'Magic Water' which allow this. This material is mixed from two resin-based components and is very runny when first mixed, taking 24 hours to set fully. Weeds, stones and reeds can all be embedded in Magic Water and the product will flow naturally around them. By adding a little white paint it can be made to look like ice if you are modelling a winter scene. Waterfalls are an interesting feature but need the water to be 'built' on the flat and added to the rocks later. Dripping taps and small springs oozing out of rocks can be made in situ as the water falling makes its own puddles by filling any hollows. Simple puddles in roads and tracks can also be made by pouring small amounts of Magic Water into depressions.

All water features seem to collect dust and need to be dusted with something like 'Pledge' furniture polish to keep them fresh.

Don Annison used ripple coat Artex with acrylic paints to create the waters for Bassenthwaite.

Magic Water sets clear and will flow round plants and rocks most realistically. Do follow the instructions very carefully!

Trees

Trees have been given a chapter to themselves as they are such an important feature in the landscape. When modelled well they really enhance a model railway; poorly done they detract from the trains.

Trees also set the season for a model railway but can be difficult to model in winter condition. It is not an impossible task as the late George Iliffe and Doris Stokes proved. More recently the creators of 'Elmwell Village' created a railway with more than one season on the same line.

There are a number of methods employed for creating realistic model trees and the relative merits of each are examined below. There are very few commercially available ready-made trees and those available fall into the following types:

1. Plastic mouldings with foam rubber leaves, the best probably being those by Woodland Scenics. The trunks (armatures) are flexible and you then attach clumps of foam rubber leaves to the branches. This is quite effective in 2mm:ft scale and okay for 4mm scale but doesn't quite work in any larger scales.
2. Bottle brush fir trees. Now whoever imagined that such a regular product sprayed green and with sawdust attached could ever achieve the suspension of disbelief test outlined in Chapter 1? The system is not beyond rescue however and a bit of work can quite quickly produce an acceptable forest to serve as the background to a railway set in the Scottish Highlands, Wales or North York Moors.
3. Fir trees made in the Far East with plastic trunks needing a little attention but quite realistic branches covered in flock for needles.

Take just one step further into the world of commercially available trees and you meet people who have made a cottage industry out of creating realistic trees. Each tree is individually created and therefore unique. Their creators use methods which are available to all amateur modellers but of course much time is saved by buying from them.

A number of methods are available to all of us, and which ones we use will depend on availability of materials and preference of the maker. Some will have more patience than others and may favour more 'instant' methods. Read all that follows and digest before making any further decisions!

There are many commercial offerings for the smaller scales, some such as Busch being quite realistic. But for a quick and economical conifer forest I could not resist these bought at an online auction from the Far East for something like 99p!

Before deciding on methods for creation of your trees you need to have worked out what sort of trees you will need for your railway. If you are modelling a particular prototype you will have to look at the trees around that location. You probably don't need to know exactly which variety they are but a general idea will be useful. Trees fall into several different categories which are grouped generally below:

1. Trees which are generally rounded, eg oak, sycamore, ash and elm (if you are modelling pre-1980 there were many more elm trees around than there are today)
2. Smaller trees such as birch, probably the easiest to model using 'seamoss', (also known by modellers as sea foam) from various suppliers
3. Tall trees, eg Lombardy poplar, quite common alongside railway lines and very tall. One that I felled in my garden was 100ft (30.5m) tall; that's 1ft 4in (400mm) in 4mm scale and a massive 2ft 4in (700mm) in 7mm scale.

Okay, so you have the patience of a saint and all the time in the world, you want the very best and will be satisfied with no less. Go to Pendon Museum and marvel at the trees created using twisted wire, come home and start work. These really are the best trees you will ever see and can be made by anyone with a reasonable amount of patience or who can organise their work schedule to minimise boredom.

My early visits to Pendon fixed the standard I wanted to achieve and I could see that their system using twisted wire provided almost every twig to which a leaf could be attached. A real tree is actually made up in a very similar way with the food supply to every twig arranged as a series of tubes made of cells which carry the sap to the leaves. However, the individual 'wires' or lines of cells are much narrower than the wires available to us. The compromise is to use copper wires from old transformer windings, or, as these are becoming rare since modern transformers have their windings sealed in plastics or shellac, try soft iron galvanised florist's wire. These are all rather soft and will not stand much handling but are best for the beginner. The very best twisted wire trees are made from steel cable, often known as Bowden cable, used as control cables in cars, garden

The oak has very many small twigs but even when it is full of summer leaves it is still possible to see through between the branches. Note the difference in colour between summer and winter grass on the roadside.

The Scots pine has a parallel, straight trunk with branches at right angles but at the top it is often twisted. In Breckland (Norfolk/Suffolk border) there are hedges of these trees which have been trimmed at about 8ft (2.4m) above ground and the branches are twisted above this height, the whole tree only being some 20ft (6.1m) tall compared to this 60ft (18.3m) example. These trees are common along the lineside not only in Scotland but also in Norfolk, Suffolk and Hampshire. Larch trees are conifers which lose their needles in winter. Their new needles in spring are a vivid green but by late summer they are similar to spruce (the usual type of Christmas tree). Their skeletons are similar but spruce, being evergreen, do not reveal theirs.

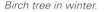
Birch tree in winter.

machinery and cycles. A visit to a repairer may yield a suitable supply. Be warned however that these wires are hard to twist and will also puncture your skin if you are not careful.

Start with a large number of wires bundled together to form the trunk. Anchor these near the base by tying with a band of the same wire. Fix these together with super glue or liquid nails from your builders' merchant before removing the wire ties. Next split the trunk into several branches. (Study prototypes of the trees you are creating.) Some types go further up than others before splitting and all split at different angles. Once the trunk is split into branches, each branch is split into smaller branches (a good rule is to halve the number of wires in each till you are down to pairs). As you split, twist the wires together (always in the same way, clockwise or anti-clockwise) as this holds the position. A drop of super glue will fix the position of each branch as you go. Tighter twisting tends towards apple trees, slightly less towards oak, lighter still towards ash and very light twisting towards willow. You really do need to look closely at the trees you are trying to copy! If you are working with very fine wire you may get more realistic results by splitting the branches the way your chosen prototype does. Some always divide into even pairs, others send out pairs of twigs at intervals up the branch.

I find this to be a really therapeutic exercise best done while watching television. It is quite satisfying to behold the creation once complete but there are further stages. A real tree will have several thousand twigs but our wire trees may have only several hundred. In 4mm scale I found it worth while adding extra twigs by gluing on small pieces of lichen. It seemed to give body to the whole tree.

At this stage the trunk needs to be 'fixed' and given body. I like to add a layer of Artex mixed with PVA with

Ash and birch have rather different shapes and branch patterns, requiring different techniques for modelling.

The Lombardy poplar is instantly recognisable but look at the diminutive size of a locomotive at the same scale! These trees are found in lines, sometimes along the side of railways, and can be created economically by using twigs from cupressus trees or the heads of pampas grass. The conifer twigs use Woodland Scenics foliage mat while the pampas grass is sprayed greenish grey and coated in Green Scene minced foam leaves. The tree in the middle is a real one.

Above: The basic toolkit for making wire trees. The wire shown here is steel cable from Screwfix, as are the end cutters. The twists need to be taken out of the cable before you can start to form up branches.

Above right: The softer alternative galvanised wire from the florists.

Left: A selection of wire trees in various stages of construction. Each has a planting 'stalk' in the centre. The conifer on the left has a trunk made from a chopstick, drilled to take the twisted wire branches.

Left: The tall ash tree twisted from steel cable now has all its twigs separated and has been given a dose of 'liquid nails' on the trunk. Push the planting spike through a piece of paper to aid forming the base of the trunk.

Below: Next, on goes the mix of PVA glue, Artex and powder paint. I mix in a jar, pour over the tree into a margarine tub then back into the jar.

suitable bark colour added in the form of poster paint or powder colour. You can paint this on or pour it over the tree (quicker but messy and wasteful).

Now to add the foliage. Minced foam rubber has become the standard since being promoted by Pendon Museum in the 1960s. You can make your own by buying upholstery foam, dyeing and mincing in a kitchen mincer (actually best to dye using enamel paint) or you can buy it in from Javis, Green Scene or Woodland Scenics. I like to spray my tree trunks a brownish, greenish grey before applying Spray Mount adhesive and then sprinkling on Woodland Scenics or your favourite foliage. Do the sprinkling over a newspaper so as to save the excess to add to the general foliage pot. For oak trees I find Woodland Scenics foliage net is effective, while sycamores (very common along railway lines as they grow quickly) are best portrayed by clump foliage. For larger scales try birch bracts (seeds) as leaves (available from Green Scene). These come in pale green but are much enhanced if dyed or sprayed a brighter green. There is a wide variety of shades of tree leaves in real life but there is the common denominator provided by the colour provided by the chlorophyll in the leaves.

These trees can be purchased commercially from Ceynix (http://www.ceynix.co.uk) and others if you don't have the time to make them yourself.

Conifer trees such as spruce and larch demand a slightly different approach. These have a straight central trunk with branches sticking out almost at right angles. To create these start with a piece of dowel or even a chopstick of about

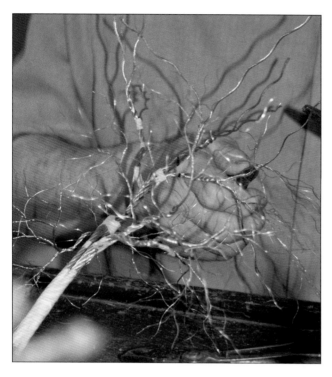

Below: Twisting and trimming a wire tree

Below left: With most of the tree now covered in gunge, if the bark gets chipped it will show a more natural colour.

Left: It is now late spring and our tree has very bright leaves in the form of minced foam from Green Scene, fixed with Spray Mount or extra hold hairspray. Can you spot the inconsistency? Yes, in the background is a field of corn being harvested in late summer (see the section on agricultural crops and seasons). By midsummer the leaves have become more dense. This is achieved with Woodland Scenics foliage net. Carefully tear off small pieces and tease out to irregular shapes and drape over the branches that have previously been covered with foam leaves.

As we pass into autumn leaves turn various shades of golden brown. This magnificent example is the creation of Charlie Shearn.

Left: The dark leaves of the conifers made by the twisted wire method contrast with the bright spring green of the willow. The pine tree and the spruce started as real twigs, shaped and drilled to take clusters of twisted wire. The Spray Mount and flock technique soon populates them with needles.

Left: A variation on the theme produces this pollarded willow, modelled on the specimens growing beside the River Cherwell in Oxfordshire. In times gone by these trees were cut down to about 10ft (3m) high every couple of years.

the right diameter for the base of the trunk. With a Stanley knife, carefully whittle the dowel down to taper it almost to a point. Use sandpaper to make it more even. Leave a scale 6ft or 2m from the base and then drill holes into the trunk to take clusters of steel wire (thicker clusters for the thicker branches near the base, single wires near the top). Superglue them in and trim any excess which pokes through using end cutters or a slitting disc in a mini drill (wear goggles as these tiny bits of wire can be dangerous). On with the Artex/PVA/poster paint mix and leave to dry before fixing the leaves. Now here is where you will see the difference between these and the

Left: Trees very often grow in groups of mixed species. This small grove of trees shows the fresh colours of late spring. Deeper into woods there is very little grass on the ground but there may be bracken or brambles.

bottle brush variety. Use Noch or Heki dark green grass flock for the needles. It may take several coats of Spray Mount but it is worth it. I have made my own flock for conifers by cutting green garden string (Nutscene) into very short lengths. It is cheap but takes for ever!

Right, so you don't have that much patience; let's look at some short cuts! Some of these have nearly as much 'wow factor' as the twisted wire trees but others are best kept for use in the background.

First off we have seamoss, often sold as 'Forest in a Box' by such as Squires and Green Scene. They come dyed a pale green but as they are very convincing as birch trees I like to spray them dark grey, which gives the right colour twigs, then splash a very light grey onto the trunks. The instructions say to attach leaves with matte medium but I prefer to use Spray Mount photo adhesive. Some prefer hairspray — experiment to find what you are comfortable with. Hold the tree horizontally and shake your chosen foliage over it, recovering the spare on a sheet of newspaper. You can enhance the look of these trees by using a slightly darker shade than you want and then lightly airbrushing a lighter shade where sunlight catches new growth. This also gives the very slight variation in colour on different branches.

Right: Seamoss, also known by modellers as sea foam, straight from the box with just a light spray of grey/brown 'plastic bumper paint'. You need to remove the seed heads and loose foliage (but save these for 'weeds').

Below right: The usual treatment with Spray Mount and moss leaves gives a very convincing tree. Seamoss is useful from 2mm to 7mm:ft scale and quickly produces a convincing forest.

Below left: Sea Moss Birch trees in autumn mode.

Below: Dense foliage is achieved by adding an additional layer.

The next 'quick fix' technique involves searching for suitable twigs from real trees. Hawthorn which has been in a hedge grazed regularly by cattle is a good source as are some twigs from pear trees (ask the owner first but be prepared for odd looks as you explain!). Some of these just need Woodland Scenics foliage mats draped over them and are a good way of making pine trees. Others can be 'fleshed out' using fibre such as cow hair, bought from a specialist plaster supplier such as Mike Wye.

You will also get funny looks if you seek out places where people have taken a JCB to the dreaded conifer hedges. Their roots often yield examples of quite realistic tree trunks. They are already the right colour and just need foliage as in the other techniques. Some heather stems can yield suitable trunks and they certainly make very realistic logs. One modeller I know uses Spirea stalks bound together to create quite large trees and he seems to make them look quite realistic

Above: How does the cow hair cling on — you've guessed it, Spray Mount!

Above right: The surprisingly realistic result after treatment with more Spray Mount and moss.

Right: This example was made from the roots of a cupressus tree. It is probably undermining the foundations of the chapel and leans too much over the roof of the adjacent house, which also has ivy growing up the walls.

Conifer roots again, but this time with clump foliage.

Grape stalks — unlikely candidates? But add clump foliage and we progress. The trees shown by the bridge on Ken de Groome's layout in Chapter 2 were created this way.

Left: This skeleton tree from an etched fret is suitable for 4mm scale but may look appropriate in the background of an O gauge layout.

but I have not been able to reproduce his results. Ken de Groome collects grape stalks and for a long time the family supplies of grapes were selected on the basis of the suitability of the stalks for making tree trunks. These need clump foliage.

I have also used heather stalks, apple and hawthorn twigs as the basis for quickie trees in conjunction with Woodland Scenics foliage net or clump foliage.

There is one more short cut to the basic tree trunk but I have only seen this once and maybe there is an opportunity for the trade to take up the idea again. This consists of an etched trunk and branches which is then covered in whitemetal to thicken it out. I suppose our Liquid Nails/ Artex methods would produce a similar result on an etch at less cost. These are best treated to Woodland Scenics foliage net.

CHAPTER 8

Man's activities in the landscape

Oxen were used for ploughing from ancient times. These were ploughing in Waldron, Sussex, circa 1910. John Hobden Collection

The farming scene

In most parts of Britain and Ireland it is the farming practices which have the greatest influence on the way the countryside looks. This is also true in most parts of Europe and parts of North America.

The author was brought up on a farm where life revolved around the shape of the land, the soil and the seasons. Each time of the year had its own jobs to be done and crops in the fields were at particular stages in their growth.

Farming practices have changed considerably over the years so it is important to consider how things were done in the period being modelled. It is very difficult to put a precise date on many of the practices common in the UK as their introduction and demise varied considerably with the type of countryside in which the farm was situated. Broadly speaking, the arable lands of the southeast have been the first to take on new technology, but even here there have been pockets of resistance, especially on small farms or in areas of marginal profitability. Likewise, machinery in particular tends to 'cascade' through the secondhand market to those areas where the profit or loss and the use of the machinery is less intense. Visitors to the Scottish Highlands and Islands will see, for example, trusty Ferguson 35 tractors ploughing and mowing on the crofts in the 21st century, these same implements having been the pride and joy of the Midlands arable farmers in the 1950s. There is no substitute for the study of photographs of a chosen area.

Tractors were first seen in Britain during World War 1. These were few and far between but by the early 1930s many arable areas were using some of the first Fordson tractors, Sandersons or Titans. The steam traction 'ploughing' engine had been used for ploughing in flat areas from the turn of the century, but its main use was as a stationary engine to drive threshing machines.

Ploughed fields are rarely modelled, yet they are seen throughout the country both in spring and autumn. This operation was traditionally the task of the teams of oxen before horses were widely employed. The last record of oxen ploughing seems to date from around the beginning of World War 1, the last strongholds being Gloucestershire and Sussex. Horse ploughing had been more usual for a century or so before this and continued to be the standard practice until about the World War 2 period. Postwar years saw tractor ploughing become normal everywhere, Tractors available at this time were the Ferguson 35, Massey Harris, Fordson Major, Allis Chalmers, Field Marshall, McCormick and Nuffield.

When ploughing a field with a traditional (non-reversible) plough the first task was to set out a marker line with the plough round the edge of the field to mark the turning space. (The headlands, or ends of the fields are always ploughed last.) This line would be 4yd (3.65m) from the edge with horses or 12yd (14.6m) with tractors, The field would then be marked out in strips of approx 30yd (27.3m) in width, varying in different parts of the country, and half of each strip ploughed one way on the outward journey, the other half ploughed the other way on the return. In wetlands the strips would be closer together and would always be ploughed the same way to achieve better drainage along the dips between each strip. When reversible ploughs came on the scene this became unnecessary as all the land could be ploughed in the same direction. The ploughs used with traction engines were the first to be reversible. These were pulled across the field between two engines and then the engines moved up a little before ploughing the next line. The amount of soil turned by a plough varied between a single strip of 9in (228mm) width for horses in heavy clay land to four strips of 10-16in (254-406mm) when tractors were used. Modern ploughs can have up to 10 shares but the norm is five.

Below: The 19th century was the heyday of the farm horse and each 'team' was in the charge of one man who had a close working relationship with his charges.

Bottom: Tractors appeared between the two world wars. The author's father is seen here c1948 with a Fordson Major and a roller.

Below: Duncan Models plough is at work here on light land. On heavier land two horses would be used.

Bottom: Plough shares turn the soil so the vegetation will rot, leaving characteristic ridges. Gulls frequently follow the plough as it turns up worms and grubs.

In the second half of the 19th century the traction engine became an important workhorse on prosperous farms.

Seed sowing in arable areas has been by seed drill since Jethro Tull invented the machine in the 18th century but backward areas sowed the seed by broadcast until World War 2. This was then harrowed into rows with a horse harrow and rolled down tight. The usual width for seed rows was 6⅞in (210mm), occasionally less. A horse-drawn drill would have 11 rows, a tractor-drawn one 20 (now some are 30 rows or more). More modern practice leaves 'tramlines' (since late 1970s) which are a pair of rows the same distance apart as tractor wheels and left as a guide for subsequent operations. The combine drill, which sows both seed and fertiliser came in about 1940. Small seeds such as grass and mustard would be sown with a hand-operated 'fiddle' drill, (seen still in use in Yorkshire 1975).

Cereal crops would be sown in early autumn or between February and March and would emerge in lines. As the crop grows it covers the bare soil so that a cereal crop resembles a field of long grass.

Grass is found everywhere but is rarely modelled accurately. Short, close mown grass is about 1-2in (25-50mm) high but left to its own devices it will grow to 2ft (610mm) high in a matter of weeks. Uniform areas of green grass are only found in specially sown fields or 'leys' where the crop is grown for hay (harvested in June), silage (harvested in May) or for rich pasture for animals. Rougher grazing land is not uniform and will usually contain a number of other plants such as docks, thistles and wild flowers such as buttercups and daisies. These may be taller than the grass and often grow in clumps. Until the middle of the 19th century the scythe was the usual tool used for cutting grass and cereals. The horse-drawn mower was usual for the next hundred years or so and then its tractor-mounted equivalent took over. To make hay the grass is raked into rows and turned every day until it can be baled. In remote Scottish crofts the hay was not baled but stacked in the fields in 'haycocks' until recent years. Bales of hay were small cuboids about 3ft (915mm) by 2ft (610mm) by 2ft (610mm) until the 1960s when large round or square bales 5ft tall were introduced. Silage is also made in bales without drying the grass. It is effectively pickled in large polythene sacks (since the1960s) but was formerly stacked in a 'clamp' or pit and taken out to feed the cattle in the winter.

For cereals harvesting the reaper and binder was the standard tool from the late 19th century until World War 2. This interesting machine had revolving 'sails' that drew the corn towards a reciprocating cutting blade and then bound the stalks into sheaves which were laid on the ground. Workers followed the machine around

the field, stacking the sheaves into 'stooks' which were left to dry and ripen further. The next stage in the process was to collect the sheaves and stack them in round stacks until the threshing machine came in the winter. These stacks were thatched to keep out the rain. The author's father continued this practice till the late 1950s on a small farm in Sussex but in the larger fields of East Anglia the combine harvester had taken over some 20 years earlier.

To model the farming practice of the 21st century requires the use of a combine harvester 36ft (11m) wide, guided by satellite navigation. Cereal crops today grow much shorter than those grown until the 1960s since the straw is no longer a useful by-product and the shorter stems are less likely to be pushed down by wind and stormy weather. Rye straw is still a tall crop, up to 4ft (1.2m) high, and there is still a little tall wheat grown for thatching.

Sugar beet is a common crop in East Anglia and parts of the West Midlands. When it was transported by rail it was also grown in Hampshire and Dorset. Potatoes are grown in rows 2ft 6in (762mm) apart and can be seen all over Britain, but concentrated in East Anglia.

The yellow fields of rape, so common in 21st century fields in April are relatively new; however, mustard, which flowers later, was common in East Anglia in earlier times.

Cabbages and cauliflowers are mainly grown in Lincolnshire and west Lancashire and can be seen all year round.

Left, top to bottom: The reaper and binder cut the corn and laid it in sheaves on the ground. There were always several workers in the field during harvest to stook the sheaves. **Bob Clements collection**

A preserved Massey Harris Combine at work.

A 36ft-cut combine needs SATNAV to steer it in a straight line!

Rape has been a common crop since the 1970s. Its yellow flowers apprear unnaturally bright. A few packets of Green Scene yellow foam should see you right for a few acres.

Below: Unusual crops can make for an interesting feature on a layout. Here bright orange pumpkins are being harvested near Wisbech.

Unusual crops

Hops are important crops in some parts of the country. These are grown up wires or poles 15ft (4.6m) tall in Kent, (Sussex until the 1930s), east Hampshire and Worcestershire. They are also grown extensively in Germany, and are common enough to feature as part of the Busch scenery range. Where hops are or were grown the farms featured the tall 'oast house' buildings with conical roofs where the hops were dried. Kent also has extensive apple orchards while Worcestershire has plum orchards, Southampton and Wisbech feature strawberry fields and the Wakefield district grows rhubarb. The Lincolnshire and Norfolk Fens grow cauliflowers and carrots. Most of these crops would be picked by hand but are now increasingly harvested mechanically. A field full of workers picking these crops, supervised by a gangmaster, would make an interesting diversion on a model.

In the early days of railways much of the land surrounding London was used for the growing of vegetables and supply of milk until the railways allowed long distance transport of such commodities. If your model is set in one of the main glasshouse crop areas such as the Lea Valley then a commercial greenhouse would make an interesting model. In more modern times a dairy or agricultural store provides extra interest and freight traffic for our models. In many parts of the American Midwest the prime purpose of the railway was to serve the grain stores which were situated every few miles along the tracks.

Animals

Farm animals need to be carefully chosen if our models are to represent a particular period, and have been the subject of unfavourable comments at exhibitions.

In the 19th and early 20th century cattle seen on farms were generally of the local breed, eg brown Sussex and Devon cows in those counties, Hereford cattle raised for beef in the Welsh border counties and Highland cattle in Scotland. Between the wars black and white Friesian cattle were introduced and gradually came to dominate the dairy herds. They were by no means universal, however, and the light brown Jersey or darker Guernsey cows were kept in many parts on Britain where they were (and still are) prized for their rich milk, high in cream content. A few farmers kept unusual breeds such as the white 'Park Cattle'. After World War 2 the Hereford was still the preferred beef breed with black Aberdeen Angus cattle gaining popularity. From the 1960s newer breeds from Europe were introduced for the beef market. These included the cream coloured Charolais and

Cows walk slowly from the dairy and generally follow each other. These Friesians are near Silverstone, Northants.

Limousin animals which dwarfed some of the smaller breeds such as Jerseys with which they were crossed. In some more remote areas the traditional breeds of cow have been kept due to their suitability to the local conditions. Thus it has often been possible to see for example Welsh cows alongside the more usual Friesians. With careful choice of models from Langley and Preiser it should be possible to create an authentic herd. For 7mm scale Duncan models provide a good older breed of cow with horns.

Wherever there is dairy farming there is a means of getting the milk to the commercial dairy. Prior to World War 2 this would have been by means of conical churns, transported in special milk wagons such as the famous GWR Siphons but each company had its own version. Milk was passenger train traffic so was generally loaded on the station platform. A group of churns was common on the platform as were baskets of other perishable traffic such as fruit. After World War 2 the churns were more cylindrical in shape and were often collected by lorry from a stand near the farm gate. The bulk milk tanker appeared in the 1970s. Let's not forget the other side of the dairy industry: the milk float with traditional bottles (available as resin castings from Langley and PLM) or the farmer with his carrier bike or tricycle delivering to just a few households. The advent of tuberculin testing in the 1950s reduced the number of farms bottling their own milk and the sign at the farm gate named the herd and proudly proclaimed the milk to be 'Tuberculin Tested'.

Breeds of sheep have been seen away from their traditional areas. For modelling purposes the Hampshire Down, Dorset Down and Swaledale sheep can be represented with the colour of the head appropriate to each but a purist would easily tell the difference in body shape. Sheep are never white but more a pale grey or cream colour except the more unusual Jacob-type with their distinctive horns. Lambs would traditionally be seen from March onwards but in recent years they may be seen from January in some areas. The shepherd traditionally stayed in the field in a shepherd's hut on wheels during lambing and could be up all night assisting his ewes. I'm not sure how to model a shorn sheep as they should be portrayed from June onwards! Sheep are marked with dye after shearing to show ownership and from September onwards the ewes may have coloured rumps to show where the ram has been at work!

To model a sheep field correctly will usually require some hurdles, used to form temporary pens while the shepherd tends to the veterinary needs of the flock

*Duncan Models
again, sprayed matt
off-white but they
would be dirtier if not
freshly shorn
(between May and
July depending on
the district and
availability of the
shearers).*

which has been gathered by his trusty, well-trained border collie dog. These are traditionally woven from hazel rods (there's a challenge for soldered wire construction) but more recently made from tubular steel.

Pigs are probably simpler to model, being predominantly pale pink Large White until 1950 but more recently Landrace and later hybrids which have leaner meat. Rare breeds such as the brown Tamworth and Gloucester Old Spot have made a comeback but are not as common as the plain variety which have been reared in fields with shelters since about 1985.

Sheep and cattle were transported in large numbers in special wagons till the 1950s. These were lime washed until the early 20th century when disinfectants became available.

Poultry was a feature of every farmyard until the 1950s. The birds would feed on scraps and grass. Some farms kept geese and ducks as well as chicken. Many households in the country kept a few chickens till about 1950 and so did railway workers who kept a few fowls in a hut on their lineside allotment. Large flocks of birds were kept in fields in the main poultry areas of Sussex, Norfolk and east Yorkshire.

Wild animals and birds

Birds are seen everywhere but rarely modelled. Most country railway stations would have a population of sparrows but these are very small and difficult to model effectively. Pigeons have always been a problem to urban railway station staff, necessitating strong control measures such as spikes on walls. These are large enough to model as are the gulls seen in most parts of the world, not just near the sea. Duncan Models provide a good representation of these for 7mm scale and Langley Models provide swans for 4mm scale; pheasants and ducks are available as castings and can be seen in many places close to railway lines.

Rabbits can be seen alongside many roads and railway lines, their population fluctuating with the incidence of myxomatosis first seen in Britain in the 1950s. Prior to that date their burrows were very common in railway embankments, slightly less so today as the animals have adapted to living on the surface where transmission of the disease is less likely than in the burrows. Castings for these are available and one layout in the 1960s, 'Ortogo', featured rabbits that disappeared into their burrows when a train passed.

Deer have become increasingly common in many rural areas and, while they flee if they see a person, they seem oblivious to the passing of cars and trains. Foxes, which were a rural animal until recent years, now inhabit many of our towns and cities. Hares, squirrels and rats are common sights in the countryside but I have never seen them modelled.

We must not forget domestic pets. Fortunately castings for these are available from many sources. Members of the modeller's family can often be persuaded to paint these non-mechanical parts of our layouts.

The rural operations associated with water also have their seasons and regional practices. In the south of England where shallow rivers flow through water

meadows the weeds would be cut in later summer after the spawning season has finished. These rivers are carefully managed as fishing rights are a good source of income. The water meadows themselves were allowed to flood in winter to allow the rich mud washed down in winter storms to fertilise the land. This provided the richest pasture and the most nutritious hay. The practice of flooding water meadows has almost died out but floods in recent years have re-created the scenes, often in summer.

The river was also important for another practice associated with agriculture, that of grinding corn. The water mill often had its own supply diverted from the main river and featured an undershot or overshot wheel beside the main building, often with the main river running beneath it. Windmills were a prominent feature in the landscapes of days gone by and can still be seen in ruins or preserved on hilltop sites. The windpump, symbolic of the American prairies, was also common in parts of England as is its modern counterpart, the wind generator. It should not be difficult to rig up a working model of these.

Other features of the rural landscape

There are a number of small features of the landscape that are rarely modelled but can contribute to the atmosphere of a railway scene and provide interest at exhibitions for those whose prime interest is not the railway. Moles are found everywhere and their distinctive mounds of earth need only a drop of PVA and some dark earth (I use liquidised peat) to create an added interest in a field. In days gone by a molecatcher would display his trophies on the nearest barbed wire fence. One feature of rural scenery which has changed very little since the dawn of the railway age is the beehive. These have always been an essential feature of orchards as the bees are necessary to ensure pollination of the fruit. They are also seen, sometimes in quite large numbers, alongside fields of beans and rape.

Arable crops were traditionally protected by scarecrows and more recently by all sorts of brightly coloured wind-operated devices. A gas-operated gun at the field edge is quite effective at scaring off birds and any passing humans.

Public rights of way through farmland leave narrow strips of ground without vegetation. These cross fences by means of stiles or 'kissing gates' which allow the passage of thin people but not cattle or sheep. In hilly areas where the animals roam common land or moorland the cattle grid allows passage of humans but deters animals. People usually walk in more or less straight lines while animals carve winding pathways to the water trough or towards the dairy. There is often a muddy patch next to the water trough or near to where cows drink from a stream or river. Cows walk in procession to the twice-daily milking. For absolute accuracy, if your operating schedule features trains through the middle of the day the cows should be grazing, the 4pm passenger should see the cows walking to or from the dairy and the 7pm might see them lying down! Farmers look after their animals' welfare and will usually provide a salt lick (pink block) in the field. A manger of hay may be provided in the winter or a line of silage spread across the field.

People

A whole industry seems to have arisen around the creation of suitable cast characters to populate our railways. They are available in all the popular scales from Springside, Dart, Langley, Andrew Stadden and others. Many of these are exquisite re-creations of famous railway engineers such as Brunel and Stroudley and are priced accordingly but other figures are available at surprisingly economical prices. Slaters Huminiatures provide a useful, if undernourished, basis for railway crowds while the ready-painted figures from Prieser can populate the railway quickly. Some Prieser figures have distinctly continental features but most are fine for UK-based situations. A recent trend has seen very reasonable ready-painted (bright and sometimes glossy) basic figures from the Far East offered on internet auction sites. These come in some unusual scales but many are appropriate for our modelling scales.

Painting people is a whole art form on its own and it is a skill which some modellers have and others don't. I like to work from photographs and I always use matt paint. As soon as I have painted a part of the figure, say a jacket or a hat, I dip it into talc (Johnsons Baby Powder or similar). This makes the paint even more matt. With animals I even work the paint again with a dry brush after application of the talc to simulate the animal's furry coat.

This Ford Model A comes from Matchbox. Its bright colour has been replaced with a spray of black acrylic car paint and the owner's name created in a word processor.

Early motor vehicles needed high ground clearance on ruted gravel roads.

Vehicles

I write as a rank amateur in the field of vehicles for there are many experts out there who are able to create authentic vehicles from specialist kits. Some of the best are produced for the car enthusiast market at 1:43 scale, 7mm:ft, correct for O gauge. Langley produce many fine cast kits for vehicles in the smaller scales with some interesting horse-drawn vehicles, lorries and tractors for 7mm scale. Duncan Models produce other agricultural and industrial vehicles for 7mm scale so there is ample available to populate any scene. Some of these kits can be pricey, reflecting the complexity of the work involved. For more economical vehicles look to the offerings of Lledo and Corgi. Some care is needed in the choice of these vehicles as they are frequently sold with no indication of scale. A search of the internet for sites selling diecast models will often give more indication of scale. A simple test by measuring the wheelbase and comparing to a full size vehicle will get you an idea of the scale. These vehicles can be picked up relatively cheaply and you can re-paint them into the colours you need. It may just be me but the photographs of, say, Ford Model T vans in the 1920s seem to show mainly black vehicles while the diecast offerings all seem rather bright. More research needed here I think, the moral being, once again, to check photographs taken in your chosen period.

Roads

One of the reasons why railways grew so quickly in the middle years of the 19th century was the state of the country's roads. In the 17th and 18th centuries roads were improved from muddy tracks by the turnpike trusts who used Macadam's system of graded stone to provide a solid surface for the horse-drawn vehicles of the time. On these roads the stones were ground together by wheels and hooves which resulted in a lot of white stone dust. This suggests that we should use very light coloured materials when reproducing them. Nigel Digby advises reading *Wind in the Willows* as a good source book for the pre-1914 era. The white dust is mentioned several times, especially in the second chapter when they go on a trip in a caravan and Toad meets a motor car for the first time! In towns a solid road was constructed from stone 'setts' or cobbles, which caused much vibration as wheels drove over them. Some of these stone roads are still in use in suburbs today, particularly in east Lancashire where roads were built at the same time as terraced houses in the 19th century. With the advent of motor vehicles tarmacadam (now made with bitumen) allowed smoother roads to be constructed. These became common after World War 1 and with the adoption of the road classification system in 1919 all A-class roads were soon surfaced in tarmac. Some country roads remained untarred into the 1960s. Some tarred roads were made by mixing small stones with the tar (or bitumen today) while others were tarred by spraying and then spreading stones on top to be rolled in. Both these processes are still in use in the 21st century. The modelling technique for making both is similar. In the larger scales spread on a layer of PVA and grey paint to the road surface (I prefer card as it is already fairly smooth). Before the glue gets a chance to skin sprinkle on fine sand and then roll it in. A toy roller is just right for rolling it in as per the prototype. For Gauge 1 and above bead blasting grit gives a good surface; for 4mm scale and below fine moulding sand works well. I collect fine sands from stream beds and where soil is washed out of fields by heavy rain and keep the different shades in jam jars until needed. If your road is a gravel one use the same technique as above except for rolling use a toy car to give the ruts you would find on such a road. Remember, though, if modelling the pre-motorised vehicle era, you will need three ruts — the centre one for where the horse walked and the outer two for the wheels of the carts.

On tarmac roads that are wide enough you will need solid or dashed white lines along the centre. These can be made from strips of off-white tissue paper glued on with dilute PVA and pressed hard into the surface. These lines were first introduced in the 1920s with the introduction of 'cat's eyes' following in the 1930s. These could probably be simulated in the larger scales using the jewels sold for lamp lenses by Langley Models. The system using double lines was phased in from the mid-1960s.

Self adhesive white lines are available from C & L Finescale.

Road signs in the form of finger posts first appeared in the 19th century. I cannot find a supplier of these but they are easy to make by soldering strips of brass to a brass tube. The lettering can be produced on a computer printer and glued on. Many other signs and posters can be produced in this way or by reducing real photographs. If you need relief to the sign then it is possible to have etchings made from your own artwork as described by Gordon Gravett in *Model Railway Journal* No 190. Warning signs are available as pre- and post-1960s in the Hornby Skaledale range.

Every county had its own distinctive design of road sign. This one outside the Star Inn, Waldron, Sussex, is typical of that county. The picture also shows a typical service manhole cover (at the foot of the signpost), an example of well-tended flower borders and the unusual English bond brickwork common in Sussex, where the headers (ends of the bricks) are grey while the main bricks are red.

Vintage vehicles add authenticity to themed days on heritage railways. Butterley station (MIdland Railway) plays host to some 1960s examples

Backgrounds

'Lydham Heath' is well known on the exhibition circuit. Barry Norman's scenery transports viewers to the leisurely world of this Shropshire backwater.

Backgrounds can be minimal or highly detailed depending on personal preferences and the needs of the railway. A few manage without them altogether. Barry Norman's 'Lydham Heath' doesn't need one as it has a dense forest of evergreen trees behind the station. Trevor Nunn's 'East Lynn' has none either; perhaps it goes with S gauge?

Beginners are probably best advised to start with one of the printed colour backscenes that are sold in model shops. Several firms make these, amongst them Peco, Townscene, Gaugemaster and International Models (UK), Walthers (USA), Faller and Auhagen (Germany) and MZZ (Switzerland). Big model shops usually have one or more of these ranges and the sheets are generally inexpensive depicting town, country or industry. Additional to these, however, it is worth looking in old colour magazines of all sorts and 'countryside' calendars for these sometimes have suitable printed scenes to the required 'eye level' viewing angle. Some backgrounds used in the 1960s were stylised, almost cartoon-like in character but they went well with the tinplate trains that were common at the time. The Peco offerings that appeared in the 1960s came as a breath of fresh air. They were (and still are) subtle with sufficient fine detail to look realistic without being 'fussy'. Faller were soon in the field with their photographic reproductions of real scenes from continental Europe. For European scenes these add much detail to any layout and can also be mistaken for scenes in the Forest of Dean where small settlements are intermingled with steeply wooded hills. Photographically produced backgrounds are also available for scenes across the Atlantic in USA or Canada from The Backdrop Warehouse:

http://backdropwarehouse.com/indexbdwh.htm

Some of these may also suit some UK or European countryside locations. They are superbly researched and photographed but they do come with a very high price tag.

The only truly UK-based photographic backgrounds come from International Models and Gaugemaster.

If you decide to make your own there are several ways to go about it.

Sky wallpaper will give a basic backdrop so that those viewing or photographing your layout do not see the operator's T-shirt between the trees and houses. This is perfect for 4mm scale, a bit small for 7mm scale and rather large for 2mm scale. It is possible to add detail to these by using photographs cut out from magazines and posters and even your own digital photographs blown up to the maximum size your printer can handle. There are pitfalls to using your own pictures as will be discussed later.

The next stage in complexity involves either painting green rolling hills onto this paper or cutting out gentle hill shapes to paste in front of it.

A fully painted backscene which can be customised to the exact features of your line is the ideal but most modellers do not have the skills to create their own so they make friends with a local artist and either commission a scene or barter for other services.

If, like me, you are up for trying your own painting then do have a go. The materials are fairly cheap so if you really don't like the result you can throw it away and go for one of the other methods. In the past such paintings, for that is what we are creating, would need to be carried out in oils. This is messy and you have to wait for one layer to dry before applying the next colour. The colours can be vibrant unlike watercolour which takes more effort to get a real depth of colour. Some people have managed watercolour backgrounds but it does seem more difficult than oils for this purpose. Fortunately in recent years acrylic paints have been widely available and these give most of the advantages of oil without any of the disadvantages. They are water based and can come as thick paste, like oils, or thin and water-like in texture. I personally prefer to use the paste-type as they do not run. They remain workable for about an hour, longer if you dilute them with PVA medium. Be careful to get matt or dull paints and medium as you do not want light reflecting off a shiny background.

The basic technique starts with applying sky colour to the majority of your 'canvas'. We do not usually use canvas but the kind of white-faced hardboard sold by all DIY shops. The sky is applied using household emulsion paint in a much lighter shade of blue than you might think. It can be applied with a brush if you are careful to smooth out brush marks, or if you have the luxury of a sprayer it is best sprayed on. A plain blue background will look very plain if it is used for any large areas so it is essential to add cloud effects. My method for this is to use an airbrush (even the cheapest Humbrol ones will do). Matt white paint is sprayed through card templates cut out into basic cloud shapes. Hold the templates about 3cm from your blue painted sky and spray very lightly through them. Next use a slightly different cloud shape and spray again to build up the colour. It should not be too thick. You may wish to add a very small amount of light grey at the cloud base but this is tricky to get right. Much more complex cloud shapes and menacing storm clouds can be built up by airbrush experts but I am writing for the jack of all trades who is prepared to experiment.

Adding the detail of the landscape comes next. If you are used to working in watercolours it may be possible work in that medium onto the prepared sky but as watercolours run you will need to work in the flat. My preference is for acrylic colours supplementing an emulsion base. As artists' acrylic colours are expensive to buy I use emulsion paint mixed up to match a particular British Standard as the base.

This simple template is used to spray through when creating clouds on a backscene.

This backscene is painted using acrylic paints. The scene is based on Weybourne, North Norfolk Railway, and you should just be able to make out the sea in the distance.

This paint is water based and will mix with the acrylic paints we will use to modify the shade. It is possible to spray these paints with an airbrush if you have that skill but as they will readily clog in the airbrush you need to move quickly and don't stop too much. I find spraying generates a lot of adrenaline but brush painting by contrast can be rather therapeutic. A couple of pieces of sponge can be helpful for adding foliage to trees. My basic emulsion colour is a grass green shade. Go to your favourite DIY store and obtain colour charts — the best are the ones which show the British Standard colours. My favourite grass shades are 2080-g30y and 4060-g50y.

First, with a soft pencil (4B sharpened to a good point) mark where your horizon will be. Also mark the outlines of significant hills. You may want to measure certain parts of the scenery on the baseboards so that your background features match or complement the foreground. For features in the far distance the green mix should be diluted considerably with blue and grey (go and look at real countryside to judge the amounts). Gradually dilute less for features close to the foreground, painting in those areas which are grass first. Next consider which areas should be painted as ploughed fields, ripening corn, unusual crops (See Chapter 8) or woodland. Paint these in using artists' acrylic paints and then add hedges and trees by adding dark brown or a little black to the basic green colour, again diluting with blue and grey in the distance. Much of the work can be done with a broad brush but smaller ones will be needed for details and I find small pieces of sponge useful for hedges and trees.

With care, photographs can be added to these scenes to show buildings but there is another technique which can enhance your backgrounds using technology if you have the necessary basic skills.

Using your computer and digital camera to produce background scenery

Railway modellers will embrace any method which enables them to produce the effects they want in their models and recent advances in technology have given us some tools that are useful, particularly in background scenery production.

Commercial suppliers have been providing backgrounds based on photographs for over 40 years (Faller etc). This technology is now available to amateur modellers with a bit of ingenuity. (If you have no computer skills at all then skip the rest of this chapter but if you have very basic skills read on!)

The first example I know of which used a digitally created photographic background was the 'Lofthouse in Nidderdale' layout created by Skipton Model Railway Society. They scanned photographs, edited them into a panorama and printed on A4 sheets to paste onto the background. You can read about it on the club website at http://www.skiptonrailsoc.org.uk/lofthouse.htm. This is a lovely line, well worth seeing if you get the chance.

In the 10 years since 'Lofthouse' first hit the exhibition circuit digital photography has moved on and is now available to all. For the first technique all you need is a digital camera (at least 5 megapixel [mP] sensor, which most are, but don't expect quality prints from a 5mP mobile phone, get a proper camera). At its simplest you just go out and take a photo or photos of a scene you want to use as your background, take the memory card to your local photo printers and ask them to print your picture as a poster. You can do this with a conventional film camera too but you are limited to the size of the poster and take pot luck as to whether the result is at an appropriate scale for your railway. With a digital camera you need some photo editing software. There are dozens of types from the commercially available Photoshop to free ones which come with your printer or scanner. If you have a good program use it; if you don't my recommendation is Serif Photo Plus at around £30. The key is to convert the file to a PDF document at a suitable size. You can download a PDF writer (eg Cute PDF writer) free. It installs itself as another printer on your system. Open your photo in your photo editing application and go to print it. Choose the PDF writer and select the paper size as A1. Your normal printer is probably A4 size but the PDF writer will allow you to print the much larger A1 size except that it will print it as a file which you save then take along on disc to your High Street photo printer and ask for a poster. This may be expensive but there are cheaper alternatives — read on. To produce your PDF file go to file-print, select printer as Cute PDF writer, go to properties and advanced options where you can select A1 size.

While you are in your photo editing software you might like to play around with such devices as copying or cloning some vegetation to cover up the 21st century road sign or other undesirable intrusions.

Another very useful device for backgrounds is software which will take a series of pictures and merge them together to form a panorama. They are cheap to buy (Serif Panorama Plus £19 if you catch them on a good day) or even free as a download. Take a series of 3 to 5 pictures as a panorama with a little overlap, import them into your software and the software will stitch them into a long thin

Right: This dialogue on the computer screen shows the process for printing your background as a very large PDF file to take to the copy centre.

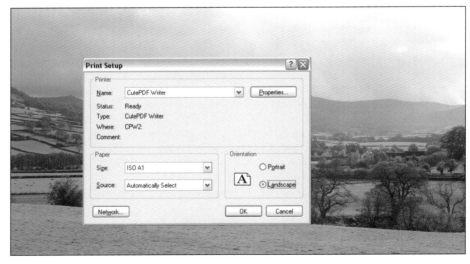

Below: Your computer generated panorama should look like this.

photo suitable as a background. The problem is finding a printer who is able to translate your masterpiece into something of a useful size.

I have spent quite a lot of time getting this technique right and can pass on the following advice.

You will need to photograph a panorama which is quite a bit longer at the base than the length of the railway it is going to be background for. I don't quite understand why but it may be something to do with the fact that most railways are compressed into a much shorter space than the prototype. You need to decide whether you want a little 'countryside' at the base and lots of sky or lots of countryside (probably in hilly areas) and little sky. Take your photos accordingly. I find a lens focal length of about 80mm (about mid zoom on most digitals) seems best and when taking the pictures keep the horizon at the same height using markers such as the focus point or any other information which appears in the viewfinder. Use a tripod if one is available as it helps keep level and avoids shake. If you find a telegraph pole in an unfortunate position you can shift your position by up to 50yd (45.8m) so that it is missed by consecutive shots. The panorama software will correct it. If you are modelling a real location you can try to capture a panorama of the background to that location. However, I have tried this for my railway and found trees and pylons in awkward places and resorted to using a scene from a few miles away which just looked right.

For a freelance line you can choose any scene in the right sort of country. The best locations seem to be from half way up a valley looking towards the other side. These can be spotted using an Ordnance Survey Landranger map and looking for publicly accessible places to take the pictures. Choose your season and weather carefully so that the images come out clearly. Bright days give best results but if you need to create an illusion of dark weather as was the case for Hull MRS layout 'Merthyr Riverside' then choose a dull day.

Getting a bit more technical you can take control of the scale of your background by importing pictures into a CAD (Computer Aided Drafting) package. If you have access to Autocad it is the best but Turbocad is reasonably priced and will let you change scale and position on the printed paper so that you can get two lengths of scene on one sheet of A1 paper.

If you are into using CAD or even simple drawing packages you can create buildings or download them from CAD libraries on the internet. These can be coloured very realistically as the users of virtual railway simulators have demonstrated. Next step is to copy your buildings (or vehicles) and paste them into your CAD drawing into which you previously imported your picture. This copy and paste facility also works in some photo editing software so there are endless possibilities. We are in danger here of letting the creation of the background scene take up more time than building the rest of the railway so do keep things in proportion. If you do really enjoy this side of things then you may give up models altogether and go 'virtual'!

One word of warning about printed backgrounds. If printed on a standard computer printer the dyes used in printing will fade on exposure to sunlight. This is probably not a problem in a loft railway but could ruin your scene if the railway

This background was generated using a mixture of photographs and CAD generated graphics. Once you have created one terraced house in a CAD programme you can multiply it very quickly and resize it to draw houses further back.

is in sunlight. The solution is to find a place that does prints using a printer supplied with pigment inks rather than dyes.

Any photographically produced background can be attached to the white faced hardboard mentioned above or to any other upright board you may have. Adding low relief buildings, trees and other details close to the background helps to blend the 3D with the flat background. The best way to attach paper to white hardboard is with Spray Mount or carpet adhesive but test a small piece first to make sure the solvent doesn't affect the inks or paints used. PVA will introduce wrinkles, however; if you are using a commercial printed background then it is worth using wallpaper paste with just a little PVA added. When it is wet the paper expands a little and then shrinks smooth and tight as it dries.

The background scene can be used to create junctions and other devices to allow some rail lines off scene into a fiddle yard or even a hidden goods yard where, for example, loaded coal wagons can be 'unloaded' and the loads transferred to the colliery at the other end of the layout (well, we are all being encouraged to recycle these days!)

To avoid a sudden change from flat to vertical scenery it is worth placing hedges, fences and trees near the backscene to break up the harsh edges otherwise created.

Here the 'Fitton End Tramway' disappears through the backscene of the 'Norfolk Joint Railway'. Its exit is disguised by trees and other foliage while the adjacent buildings focus the viewer's attention away from the disappearing line.

On the Midhurst branch, created by members of the Leyland Model Railway Club, very effective use is made of the background to allow various branches to duck in and out of the scene presented to the public.

Creating the final scene, grouping and placing buildings and creating cameos

In Chapter 1 mention is made of the practice of the great artists to divide their pictures into distinct scenes, each of which might make a picture or cameo in its own right. We can do this in our models too but we have to balance our desire to create these scenes in a way which is pleasing to the viewer with the need to follow the way the prototype is laid out. Fundamental physical principles such as water always flowing downhill must be adhered to and we must take account of such things as the dynamics of people movement. For example, when setting out a station forecourt, check if vehicles can physically enter it without reversing. Ask how the miniature people who would be using our railway would go about their daily model lives. What facilities would they need and what guidance does study of the prototype give us in positioning them relative to other features?

Older buildings and features may appear to be scattered around the countryside at random but in fact there are reasons for the placing of every one. In earliest times settlements were constructed where there was a good water supply, but on higher ground to avoid flooding. Communal systems of farming meant people lived in groups or tribes and the settlements started before the Norman conquest of Britain (the majority of villages in fact) clustered about a village green, river or trading route. Look for names ending in -ing, -ham or -ton (Saxon origin) -thorpe or -by (Viking origin) -chester or -caster (Roman). The original buildings have long since gone but more recent ones have been built on their sites. In villages these are usually well spaced with gardens but in towns the pressure on land has led to every space being filled with unplanned clusters of buildings of different ages.

With the coming of the industrial revolution and the railways came more planned towns, straight lines and terraces of houses, all built in a short space of time. Many older buildings in town centres were demolished to make way for bigger shops. A useful way to complete the railway scene is to build a typical 'Station Parade' with a row of shops and perhaps a hotel built where they could take advantage of the people passing to get to the station. These can be built in low relief (frontage or backs only) so only half the work to do.

This cluster of buildings in Hastings, Sussex, were built piecemeal between about 1600 and 1800. Behind is the gable of a typical Victorian seaside house with a chimney pot to serve the fire in every room.

The placing of vegetation around buildings is also important in setting the scene and making it look realistic. Study photographs and see how village buildings relate to the trees around them.

Above: In the countryside few buildings are arranged in straight lines. Clusters are far more frequent, as here at Bowland Bridge in the Lake District.

Right: Runswick Bay, North Yorkshire, is a very tightly packed village clinging to its steep sided valley. This would make a very suitable subject to model in perspective.

Terraces near Ebbw Vale. The coming of railways, mines and factories created a demand for mass housing, often laid out in rows or terraces.

Creating cameos, dioramas and stories

When modelling a prototype location you will, during the course of your research, come to learn a lot about the history of the location, why the railway was built and how it came to be sited as it is. Stations were sometimes built away from the settlements they served either for geographical reasons (town too high on the hill, too far away to divert the main line) or if a local landowner did not want the line passing in front of his manor house. For a fictional location it is worth creating the story as this will help to determine where roads would be needed and help to link industry with the settlement. The story can also be used to explain junctions that are really only there to help make operation interesting. Many model railways make use of planned lines that were never built. Real towns can be re-created as a background to fictional lines. Remote seaside villages can be elevated to major resorts 'if the railway had been built'.

Below are some of the mixtures of fact and fiction that I have employed on my 'Norfolk Joint Railway'.

Banningham

The real Banningham is a very small village near the M&GNR in Norfolk. There was never a station to serve it but I have made it the junction of a fictitious branch from Cromer, assuming the Norfolk & Suffolk Joint Railway was never built. The station is built in the style of the N&S Joint but the buildings that form 'Banningham Street' are drawn from attractive examples all over East Anglia. Businesses have typical Norfolk names and there are relationships which explain their presence. Arthur Marsham was a cobbler who always wanted a shop so he built a shack on a bit of open ground next to the chapel.

One day in early July 1937 Arthur was walking past Jabez Benstead's Banningham New Mill (a steam mill) when he spotted smoke coming from the railway near Tony Cooper's field. He leapt across the fence, startling the pheasants, ran across the light railway to the main line and started to stamp out the fire with his feet. He couldn't stop the fire but managed to keep it out of the ripening wheat till Tony's men arrived with shovels to complete the job. Tony 'deent arf cuss' but thanked Arthur for his swift action. A reminder of the day was found in the form of a snapshot in Arthur's photo album when he passed away in 1992.

The fire by the side of the railway near the junction with the 'Fitton End Light Railway' was extinguished just in time to protect the ripening wheat, seen here being gathered by Tony Cooper's men. Today it is likely that this operation would be carried out by just one operator.

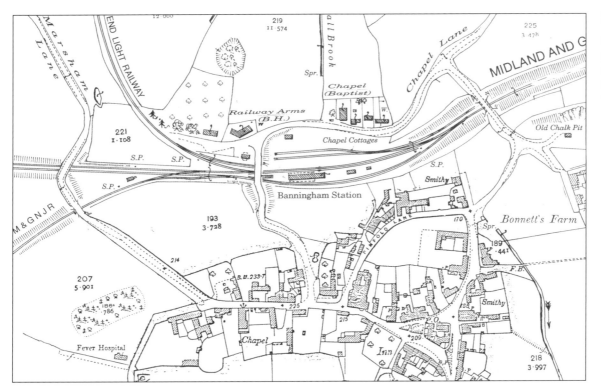

Banningham station was never recorded on the Ordnance Survey maps but a little bit of cut and paste work provided a suitable plan which was shown to Roger Fairclough, the curator of the Map Room at Cambridge University Library to test its believability. Roger looked carefully and pronounced that it must be somewhere in Norfolk but that it was an odd plan as it had typefaces in both 1887 and 1906 styles!

Fox Cottage

I was first attracted to this building in 1980 as I drove past and saw it featured a mixture of light red Norfolk brick, carrstone and chalk under a slate roof. It had originally been a single storey building and probably thatched but signs in the gable end showed that it had been extended to make it two storey. Its slate roof dated this to a time after the railway had arrived in the district in 1846. How would you have got slates into East Anglia from Wales before that? I photographed it and made a sketch to scale without any measurements. It was clear that this was a subject for card modelling and so I set about scribing all the various parts. I set it into its scene next to Banningham station in 1982 and moved it in 1996 when the whole railway was re-located. At that time there was an opportunity to create the field next to it so trees and hedgerows were added, mainly from foam and, to add interest, a fox was placed in the field.

Fox Cottage is one of the group of buildings which make up the fictional part of Banningham's street. It is older than the others which were built after the railway came. This cluster softens the edge to the backscene.

The Railway Arms. Later in the day there is more work for PC Plod as one of the customers of the Railway Arms (based on Yarmouth's White Swan) seems to be drunk in charge of his bicycle.

In 2004 at work I received a phone call asking me to go and do some drawings of the building. When taking down the address I knew the number and the road name but the owner then said, 'It's actually called "Fox Cottage" ...'. Scary! But it served to illustrate what I should have realised: that every building or locality is named after some person or event of real significance locally.

When creating cameos they may be linked to other scenes and should be consistent in their stories but do remember the advice in Chapter 1 and keep each one discrete as its own self-contained picture. What can you say about your railway which explains its features and makes it believable?

The advent of DCC control of trains has re-awakened interest in the use of sound to enhance model railways. The ability to record sounds and program them for any model purpose is now within the grasp of most teenagers — adults take a little longer to get to grips with it but why not apply the technology to scenery? Possible projects include church bells, maybe a wedding would be too twee for a model railway, cows and sheep, signal bells, crossing sirens and platform announcements. Some interesting lighting effects such as welders, glowing incinerators and bonfires can be combined with sounds to create interest when there are no train movements. When this is done well the effects are carefully controlled as to their timing and duration so as to prevent them being an overload on the senses.

Covering the joins, physically and by illusion

Real life scenery passes from one phase to another fairly seamlessly and obvious changes such as the last house in town will have a transition such as a garden. We may create our cameos away from the baseboard and only place them together as they are completed. There is much to be said for this as it allows us to work at a bench or table seated in comfort. We need to plan how to blend the pieces together. We need to attempt to place joins where they will be least noticeable such as beside hedges or walls. For exhibitions where baseboards are split and reassembled for each show some builders simply place additional scatter material

The Banningham Estate keeper on his rounds with his dog.

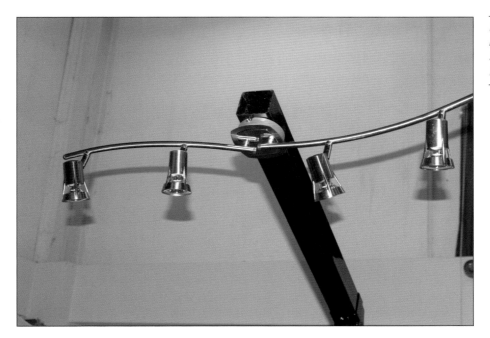

Prototype lighting rig being developed by St Neots Model Railway Club.

across the joint. I have also seen a railway where a strip of polythene was stuck to each baseboard edge and the ground cover material glued down right across the join with PVA as usual. When the boards were split and the glue dry the polythene had not stuck to the PVA and so peeled off easily. The resulting join was almost invisible. The placing of a large foreground object across a join will conceal the join behind it.

Some railways have branch lines leaving the main baseboard to go to a fiddle yard or another board. The classic way to leave a baseboard is by way of an overbridge or tunnel. If it is a tunnel then remember to take the dark lining well off scene and if it is a bridge then create some green scenery on the other side so that viewers do not see too much of the operators' hands, tea cups or screwdrivers. Having the line go into a cutting or behind a building works well and you can even use a line of trees to disguise the exit.

Other illusions can include the placing of a prominent feature such as a signalbox to divert attention from the join or exit or even, if you have lighting, the area being less well lit than the rest of the line. Lighting model railway scenery is a subject in itself, with some brief notes appearing below, but in this chapter let me just sow a few seeds to give food for thought.

Some railways incorporate lighting which can change from day to night or from sunshine to cloud. This can be a great enhancement to the viewer's enjoyment of the scene and the establishment of the desired atmosphere so for a few pounds' worth of equipment it is possible to add considerably to the effect.

Many exhibition layouts have elaborate lighting rigs taking some time to erect. These can have substantial posts at the front of the railway, needing care to avoid them being in the view. Others have their lights on arms stretching over from the back of the layout. St Neots Model Railway Club have developed a system using square rainwater downpipes and their joints as the lightweight girders and running the wires inside them. Four mini spotlights are mounted on each.

The other decision to make is the type of light. Fluorescents are powerful, cheap and even but tend to give a cold light. Tungsten lamps are warmer and give off heat but it is difficult to control shadows. The new low energy lamps are cold like fluorescents. To light extensive scenery well needs the most even coverage possible. Parts of a scene which are darker than others do not look like clouds passing, they look odd. Shadows are fine if the light is even. Nigel Digby's solution is to have several spotlights each pointing the same way, to emphasise the direction of the sun.

Appendix 1 – Suppliers

Traditionally, model railway suppliers operated from high street shops and by mail order. Increasingly, online shopping shows no postal address for suppliers. Accordingly, in this list, there is a mix of postal addresses and website addresses.

To see the products and judge for yourself, look out for traders' appearances at exhibitions.

Realistic tree kits —
http://www.treemendusmodels.co.uk or www.ceynix.co.uk

Trees, textures and backgrounds - International Models, North Wales www.internationalmodels.net

Card buildings — http://www.superquick.co.uk

Downloadable buildings and brickpapers in several scales — http://www.scalescenes.com/

Card building kits by Bilteezi, Howard Scenics and Prototype also backgrounds — Freestone model accessories — Mail order and exhibitions only 28 Newland Mill, Witney, Oxfordshire , OX28 3HH

Card building kits, OO / N — Metcalfe, Bell Busk, Skipton, North Yorkshire , BD23 4DU

Raggs to Riches American buildings — http://www.ngtrains.com/

Embossed plastic brick – www.slatersplastikard.com

Balsa and card canal boat kits, and lock gates, OO — http://www.garthallan.co.uk/kits.htm

Fine detailed castings Dart Castings / O from Craftline — http://www.dartcastings.co.uk

7mm scale agricultural and other accessories, Duncan Models, 34 Waters Road Salisbury Wilts SP1 3NX Tel: — 01722 321041. www.duncanmodels.co.uk

Etched windows —
http://www.gtbuildingsmodels.co.uk/ and http://www.brassmasters.co.uk

Resin windows — www.portwynnstay.co.uk

Commissioned buildings and brick/stone papers, bridges www.kirtleymodels.com

Textures, scatters, trees and more — Green Scene www.green-scene.co.uk

Trees and foliage, Woodland Scenics, available from Bachmann — http://www.bachmann.co.uk

Busch Scenics — http://www.busch-model.com/english.htm

Faller Scenics from —www.modellandscapeco.com

Magic Water — http://www.unrealdetails.com

White metal details (huge range in all scales),Langley — www.langley-models.co.uk

Plastic building kits, N, Kestrel — http://www.north-london-models.com

Dapol plastic kits, N / OO — http://www.dapol.co.uk

7mm footbridge — http://www.cockothenorth.net

Ratio and Wills accessories and materials, available from Peco — http://www.peco-uk.com/

Resin and plaster cast accessories, Ten Commandments — www.cast-in-stone.co.uk or PLM Cast-A-Ways 12 New Street, Merry Hill, Wolverhampton, West Midlands , WV3 7NW

Tunnel Mouths — http://www.gaugemaster.com or http://www.thebradnorbranchline.co.uk

Cast Accessories, Dart Castings — www.dartcastings.co.uk

Etched components, Scale link — www.scalelink.co.uk

Old plans of stations — http://www.old-maps.co.uk

Also look for alternative suppliers at — www.ukmodelshops.co.uk or in current model magazines

Further reading and inspiration

Landscape Modelling, Barry Norman, Wild Swan 1986

In Search of a Dream (the story of Pendon Museum), Stephen Williams (Ed), Wild Swan 2007

Right Track Videos Nos 5, 6 and 7, Barry Norman and Geoff Taylor, BRM

How to Build Realistic Model Railroad Scenery, Third Edition, Model Railroader Books

Cottage Modelling for Pendon, Chris Pilton, Ian Allan

The Art of Weathering, Martyn Welch, Wild Swan 1993

And of course the many model railway magazines in which articles on scenery construction have appeared.